LOTUS ESPRIT

Osprey AutoHistory

LOTUS ESPRIT

Mid-engined S1, S2, S2.2, S3 & Turbo

JEREMY WALTON

First published in 1982 by Osprey Publishing Limited
27A Floral Street, London WC2E 9DP
Member company of the George Philip Group
First reprint autumn 1983
Second reprint spring 1985
Third reprint spring 1986

United States distribution by

Publishers & Wholesalers Inc
Osceola, Wisconsin 54020, USA

British Library Cataloguing in Publication Data
Walton, Jeremy
    Lotus Esprit.
    1. Lotus automobile—History
    I. Title
    629.2′222   TL215.L67
ISBN 0-85045-460-3

Editor Tim Parker
Associate Michael Sedgwick
Photography Mirco Decet
Design Fred Price

Filmset and printed in England by
BAS Printers Limited, Over Wallop, Hampshire

Contents

Prelude

A British genius. Anthony Colin Bruce Chapman CBE, RDI BSc (Eng), FRSA, was born May 19 1928. His career encompassed service as an RAF pilot as well as employment in development engineering for British Aluminium before the official foundation of Lotus Cars in 1951. Nobody has done more to raise the standard of creative development in racing and sports motoring over the last three decades

The mid-engined Lotus Esprit was a familiar concept to Lotus Cars when it was launched with a Paris preview of its Giugiaro-inspired and Chapman modified lines. That was October 1975, and the car was still two months from the initial pre-production stage that preceded genuine series manufacture from June 1976 onward. Since then a total of over 2350 have been made in four normally aspirated series (S1, S2, S2.2 and S3) with the top of the range Esprit Turbo leading a strong production renaissance at the Hethel, Norfolk factory when these words were researched.

The background to the Esprit's conception is fascinating in the way that almost every story connected with Lotus appears to be. The factory management are unusually frank and if this story has more than the usual 'warts-and-all' feeling about it, I must acknowledge that this is because Lotus have always allowed the kind of open and flexible relationship with a writer that is often only possible with a smaller manufacturer. Over the years I have been particularly fortunate in my contacts with Mike Kimberley (Managing Director, Lotus Cars Ltd.) and Sales Director Roger Putnam. The bulk of straightforward technical comment comes from conversation with Tony Rudd, now Corporate Research Director, but also respected for his engineering past with Rolls-Royce and BRM.

Enthusiasm for Lotus as a marque is inevitable from any spirited driver, but what we have seen in recent years (since the 1974 launch of the first 16-valve, 2-litre Elite—first of the 'new' Lotus

6

upmarket range) has been a determined effort by Lotus to get away from their racing and kit car origins and establish themselves as purveyors of exciting, yet refined, high performance machines.

The latest range of Esprits, S3s and Turbos, with their common chassis and suspension re-vitalisation, have done much to confirm that it is within the grasp of Lotus to fulfil founder Colin Chapman's aspirations to become a genuine British alternative to Porsche or Ferrari. Chapman is not just content with a 1960–1981 Grand Prix record that reads Lotus, 71 wins; Ferrari, 52 and Porsche 1.... Of course Ferrari did win another ten Grands Prix between 1950 and 1960 and Porsche would probably riposte, 'how many times have Lotus won Le Mans?' But the fact remains, of the modern constructors at the pinnacle of motor racing, Lotus has an unmatched record, including seven seasons as world champion constructors, the last in 1978. It is a heritage to be proud of, but not

Home for Lotus road cars and associated engineering and engine manufacture since 1967 has been the Hethel site. Team Lotus operates separately and there are other converted hangars there to accommodate future Lotus engineering. The factory stands on a 55 acre site and has included a body laminate division since 1970, with production of the 16 valve 900 series of motors opening in 1971. An emission laboratory became operational in 1974.

All Esprits are made here, the facilities including 278,000 sq ft of factory space, some 26,000 sq ft of open plan offices and a 2.4 mile test track, the last a fast circuit converted from past use as an aerodrome

one that I found Colin Chapman wanted to harp on when I was privileged to interview him in the late seventies.

Chapman left me literally dazed with his sheer enthusiasm for today and tomorrow, not Old Glory. The Esprit represents part of Colin Chapman just as has every product since those original trials and racing cars. One of the most interesting facets of writing this book was to learn how he and Giorgio Giugiaro did actually roll up their sleeves and work the inevitable problems out together, in the Lotus company flat beside Turin's River Po during the gestation period Giugiaro's second Esprit prototype. . . .

Mike Kimberley and Colin Chapman pose with the elegant original Giugiaro Esprit. The spirit was right, but the details, particularly for practical production, took inspiration and hard work to produce a saleable road car

Chapter 1
Origins

Lotus Cars Ltd. was formed in 1951, its initial experience with mid-engine layouts coming from feedback from Team Lotus and their $2\frac{1}{2}$-litre Coventry Climax-powered Lotus 18, which was also produced for customers in Formula 2 ($1\frac{1}{2}$ litre) and Formula Junior (1.1 litre) guises after the 18's 1960 introduction. Its place in Lotus history? Providing the first GP wins in 1960, as well as their first race-productionized mid-engine layout.

The first Lotus mid-engined road car was a bold international venture and one of the very first serious attempts to bring the proven handling advantage of the mid-engine to a wider range of customers. The car was appropriately called the Europa, and it was launched in 1966 with the Renault 16 alloy engine and transaxle. Like any true Lotus it was to become legendary for its handling capabilities, guided at then phenomenal cornering trajectories with fingertip pressure.

By 1971 the Europa publicly received the benefit of Tony Rudd's attention (he had joined Lotus in 1969), gaining the Big Valve version of the Lotus-Ford Twin Cam engine and becoming 'about the quickest thing from A to B there was . . . and *very* economical', in Rudd's recollection. He had, however, the honesty to shudder at the memory of the constant gear linkage and change problems they suffered throughout the Europa's

Above *Present day Director of Vehicle Engineering, Colin Spooner, who had responsibility for the Esprit project*

life. In fact the present Director of Vehicle Engineering, Colin Spooner, a key figure in Esprit development along with Lotus stylist Oliver Winterbottom, advised me that the quality of gearchange was always an Esprit priority after the Europa's unreliable linkages.

Naturally it was from the Europa that inspiration for the Esprit sprung, particularly as the older model had always proved the most popular of the Lotus range in America with 80 per cent of all sales. The Esprit has repeated the pattern in that market, 'with Turbo variant ascending as a proportion of Esprits in the UK, all the time', in Mike Kimberley's words. By that time (January 1982) some 173 Esprit Turbos of the original Essex and later series had been made.

Tony Rudd arrived at Lotus from BRM in 1969, charged with the responsibility of creating the new Lotus four cylinder, 16-valve engine, Type 907. It was the creation of 907 engine too, for Rudd had to buy the tooling to make the motor as well as supervise its development.

By July 1970 Rudd had the engine programme sufficiently under control to take on a wider look at future Lotus Cars activity with the objectivity of a recent recruit. 'I was told by The Chairman [the way management refers to Colin Chapman: sometimes it's just 'The Old Man', but always with respect!] to draft for Board approval a long range programme. Included in that forecast was the M70: all our programmes have a coding and this referred to the Project Number, *not* the Lotus Type Number of the vehicle. As I remember it my wording referred to a wedge theme to the styling and its role as a Europa replacement using as many parts of the M50 (Elite) as possible, including the engine,' said Rudd to set the scene.

Both M70 and M71, the latter a projected V8 version of Esprit, received Board approval in

1970, but no firm start date for work to commence was given. It was and is normal Lotus practice to review new projects every three months to see if they should be implemented and be allocated money and men. The new Elite and 1971's production of the 907 engine—then rated at 140 bhp—for Jensen took up most of the limited resources available within the car group.

Spring 1971: Colin Chapman is attending the international Geneva motor show, a traditional curtain-raiser to the European car show year. He is approached by Giorgio 'Giorgetto' Giugiaro, perhaps the most internationally influential of Italian stylists today through his firm, Ital Design, a team which has produced the basic concepts for so many attractive production cars of the seventies and eighties.

Giugiaro has a genius for bodywork of all types that echoes Chapman's intuitive engineering ability to set the pace on the track and for the road. Born in 1939 in the province of Cuneo, Giugiaro began his styling career within Fiat's central office in 1956. By 1960 his talent had been recognised at Bertone, where he created outlines like those of the BMW 3200 CS and Fiat 850 Spider, amongst others. For five years the young Giugiaro brought new respect to the Bertone name. He left for Ghia in 1965, but even a senior position in that outfit, now a Ford subsidiary, was not enough. In 1969, with partners Aldo Mantovani, Luciano Bosio and Gino Boaretti, he founded Ital Design. Perhaps their best known touring bodies of today are the Golf and the Alfasud, but Ital were also responsible for the current, sportier Alfetta GTV/GT coupés and the original VW Scirocco.

Giugiaro simply told Chapman he would like to exercise his talents on a Lotus—a compliment in itself to the company's growing international

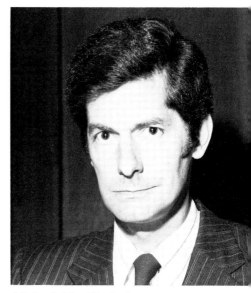

Michael John Kimberley, C Eng, MMechE. Flying to Japan or discussing a wishbone modification, it could be said that the lanky Mr Kimberley has one of the most demanding jobs in the British motor industry

Left top Former BRM racing team engineer and designer Tony Rudd, who came to Lotus in the same year as Kimberley, charged with engines engineering responsibility

11

The mid engine Europa in later Big Valve Twin Cam form. Launched in 1971 and made until 1975, the Twin Cam model was priced just under £2000 in the year of its announcement and was widely regarded as the epitomy of economical cross-country travel at the highest speeds. The Europa was always the most popular model in America

prestige. Chapman recalled the M70 project, and what I understand to have been 'a very special deal', was arrived at. Not for Lotus the kind of Lire invoice that might have occupied two cheques!

Rudd recalled for me that the first car, known within the factory as 'the Silver Car' was based upon 'a diabolical cut and shut Europa chassis. It was wider and longer than a Europa, to the planned M70 dimensions, with the wheels and tyres we wanted to use, plus the 2-litre engine and a sort of filigree arrangement to illustrate what the gearbox would look like. We hadn't got one of those, because we had yet to get to thinking about that ...' said Tony Rudd with a broad grin

spreading beneath the shock of greying hair and sturdy glasses.

The result amounted to a rolling platform on which Giugiaro could illustrate his talent while Messrs Kimberley and Rudd scoured Europe for a gearbox to suit their needs.

Although they knew that production of the Citroën SM, that exotic Maserati V6-engined device, was soon to cease, Citroën were able to offer Lotus a deal on their five speed unit destined to last for a decade. For the Lotus it would be turned the other way about, the SM being front wheel drive in the Citroën tradition, which led to an amusing late pre-production story from Colin Spooner. 'We got right up close to our target

One of the most controversial sports cars ever sold on the British market was the Jensen Healey. It and the Lotus 16-valve engine got off to a bad start with a considerable oil consumption problem that finally demanded a solution from Tony Rudd's engineers to remedy the matter. Compared to the final Big Valve specification of 'Ford' Twin Cam, as used in Europa and Elan, the Type 907 produced 140 bhp from 1973 cc instead of 126 bhp from 1558 cc

13

Lotus optimism about the clientele and carrying capacity of their first Type 907-powered road car, the front engine Elite, is well reflected in this catalogue shot. The Elite was launched in 1974 with the 2 litre 907 engine officially rated at 160 bhp. Reflecting the nature of this car compared with previous Lotus is the list of standard/optional equipment over the years

production dates, working along the assumption that we would have to machine our own crown wheel and pinion assembly because of turning the gearbox round. In fact, if we had installed that CWP the only effect would have been to give the Esprit five reverse gears and one forward, for it was not until a very late stage that we found the Citroën Maserati engine ran *backwards*, so there was no need to change CWP!'

Citroën were very co-operative over the question of gear ratios too. Lotus were able to pick the ones needed for this application, ratios that have been used ever since and also used on the Turbo, but mated to differing tyre sizes and a one-inch increase in diameter. When Lotus had picked the ratios, Citroën ensured they were cut using their tooling. Writing in the early eighties I was told that there was 'reasonable security of supply', so far as the SM gearbox for the Esprit was concerned, but it was known that Citroën were not satisfied about the strength of the gears to withstand Turbo application, never mind the rumoured 330 bhp of the Lotus V8, or more precisely the literally doubled torque value of the eight.

As an installation the gearbox/transaxle is far from straightforward and breaks 'every known engineering law', according to one executive with whom I discussed the matter. Lotus have to split every unit that arrives at the factory, install their driveshaft bearings and make the connection (a straightforward North–South installation) between engine and transaxle, via a Lotus bell housing.

Giugiaro had the original Silver Car in display, rather than running, trim during 1971 and it caused a sensation wherever it was seen, not least inside Lotus. 'Nice—but how do we get it out of our body moulds?' (strongly akin to die casting moulds in principle), was the main company question. Essentially Giugiaro had established the Esprit theme, though that was not its name at the time. The swoopy body was, however, not totally practical to make and looked as though it might present aerodynamic problems.

To investigate their needs further, Lotus took the concept and turned it into a quarter scale model for MIRA wind tunnel examination. Sure enough there were lift problems with the original shape. To get it right would demand an extraordinary effort, both from Lotus management and Ital Design.

Basically they committed themselves to the manufacture of a second prototype, complete with opening doors and fully styled interior, with a chassis underneath that was very much the test model of the actual M70 backbone unit, rather than a cut-and-shut Europa unit. Oliver Winterbottom would supervise the construction of this second, far more practical, version whilst living within that temporary company accommodation in Turin.

Yet, as the 'Red Car' proceeded it was not just Oliver Winterbottom who represented Lotus on the spot. Mike Kimberley takes up the tale: 'it seemed to go on forever. Once, twice, sometimes (rarely) even three times a week we would fly down, myself and The Chairman. We had some really epic flights to and fro, including one occasion where the plane didn't have oxygen and had to fly between Alps to keep the occupants conscious. It made a pretty long day, especially after the trip without oxygen. Then we landed feeling a bit sleepy and still had a full day to do.

'My best memory of that period was of working late at the styling studio and seeing both Colin and Giugiaro spark off each other to get the windscreen right. It was raked about 22° on the original and we felt it had to be more upright for impending legislation on visibility. The problem was how to keep the rakish look and be legal.

'Giugiaro was literally in there with bits of plaster modifying things as we went along, but it just didn't look right. Finally Colin came up with the idea that we leave the centre of the screen where it was permissible for legal reasons and move the outer bottom screen edges forward, giving us a 'fast' A-pillar line. It was the sheer inspiration of two really original minds feeding off each other that produced the answers on that car.'

The resulting Red Car carried the show registration I DGG 01 and was notable also for having the radiator in a pod beneath the bumper

Right Esprit has two front engine brothers, the Elite (top) and the Eclat, which differs primarily from Elite in having a marked sloping roofline at the rear and a generally lower level of equipment with corresponding price adjustment. Both Elite and Eclat shown here are of the 2.2 litre series, their engines shared with Esprit. It was from these models that Lotus drew the front suspension for the S3 and Turbo Esprits

The original chassis for Esprit, front end closest to camera, was used for all models up to and including Esprit S2.2. The principles were typical of previous Lotus practice, a single backbone linking front box-sectioned suspension and radiator mounting points with the tubular engine cradle at the rear. The use of box sections to strengthen the basic structure is also typical

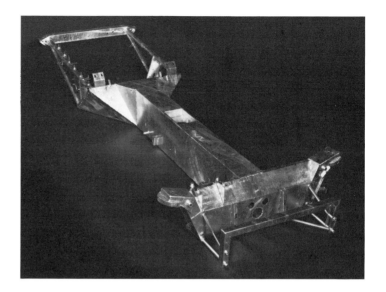

rather than the original bonnet-vented line of the first Esprit. 'The command module' principle of the instrument pod was all there to see, as was the much squarer line and careful 'productionization' of the body to suit Lotus capabilities. Still the car had no name. . . .

It had to begin with E . . .

Giugiaro had set his heart on another name in the Ital series referring to long nose styling: Kiwi. Lotus had an equal tradition of starting their modern production cars with an E—Elan, Europa, Elite (twice), Elan 2+2 and so on. Rudd recalled, 'we pointed out to Giugiaro that Kiwi might be fine in Italy, but in Britain it meant a brand of boot polish in most people's minds!' A weekend with a dictionary and a number of volunteer searchers produced the name which Rudd remembers as having gone for approval with 'virtually no dissent: Esprit'.

The Red Car was ready for detailed exam-

The 'Red Prototype,' second Lotus-Giugiaro collaboration on Esprit lines faithfully predicted how the Esprit would look, right down to the Wolfrace wheels. There were detail differences—like the chrome petrol filler caps instead of production fibre glass units for example—but the basic shape has slipped through the years attracting favourable comment

ination in the later part of 1973. Commented Rudd, 'the project was moving along well but rather overshadowed by the engine side of the business and the pressing priority of getting Elite out . . . at our third attempt!'

Easter 1974 and the structure of Lotus Cars itself altered. Mike Kimberley became chief engineer in 1974 and managing director, former Ford boss Sir Leonard Crossland became Vice Chairman with a responsibility for management technique, something hitherto lacking in a strongly engineering-orientated firm, while Tony Rudd was accountable for all new projects.

Rudd's first new assignment was the M70 Esprit. Now there was a growing impetus behind the car, for the Europa was running out of emission and crash testing time on the USA market. Between 1966 and 1974 some 9230 Europas were made, so that by the summer of 1974 there was a pressing need for Lotus to get their mid-engined act back together for the US market—and fast!

Chapter 2
A runner-sprinting to a schedule

So it came to pass that Tony Rudd recruited a basic half dozen to trek with him from the mirror-windowed delights of Hethel for the secrecy of Ketteringham Hall, a site now more familiar as the base for Lotus Grand Prix activities, but then devoid of such glamorous associations. Mr Rudd was charged with many forward assignments, but the priority was to take the Esprit and make it work. The target? It was to be a runner for Christmas 1974.

Colin Spooner had already carried out some detail design work on the concept at Hethel, so they knew there were going to be detail differences between Giugiaro's Red Car and the running prototype that would illustrate their ideas in motion. For example, the petrol filling arrangements moved from a filler just inside the rear window to the external types seen on the current model, and so on.

Tony Rudd remembers his team well today— and so does the company, for all were still working there in 1982. All had earned promotion, much of it directly attributable to their performance on the Esprit project.

A prime example of this was Rudd's 'pretty

Above *Lotus claim to make over 63 per cent of their cars themselves and this is the heart of the matter, fabricating and welding the steel chassis at Hethel*

Left *The message is simple, but Lotus management— including Colin Chapman— spent many hours refining the Italian maestro's masterpiece*

21

Above *Original front suspension, which was retained on all models up to and including S2.2, was this Opel Ascona based double wishbone layout. It amounted to a complete Opel front corner, but with Lotus springs and dampers and appropriate geometry for its new home*

Right *Running gear ready. The original Esprit in production at Hethel in 1976 with the single box section rear suspension arm and lower link, added after prototype experience, clearly visible*

Far right *Esprit engine with its new bellhousing to mate with Citroën SM five speed transaxle (closest to camera). Note also the oil cooler location to the right of the picture and the use of inboard rear disc brakes*

fierce secretary', Chris Wynder. Today she is back working for Rudd, but this time as a senior buyer, a position in which she is 'simply superb; a talent she first showed in chasing Esprit along', in Rudd's words.

Colin Spooner took responsibility for the chassis and body. His brother Brian Spooner adapted the Citroën transmission to its new task, also executing the hubs and some suspension parts. Tony Rudd laid out the basics of suspension, 'with bits of black cotton and a table to get the layout!'

Transferring their work into metal and fibreglass were Charlie Prior (pattern maker) looking after the body moulding; Ted Fleet, a fitter who looked after the Esprit chassis, and Dennis Jewell, a vehicle fitter who put the ensemble together.

They had a vehicle to show Colin Chapman by

This picture is solemnly dedicated to showing that the sparks always fly at Lotus! Chassis fabrication, Hethel-style

Christmas Eve 'but there were a few problems', admitted Rudd. 'Like the instrument cluster from French Talbot, by Veglia, which was lost on the railways, and so on. It was agreed we would stand down in the early hours and that I would meet Mr Chapman at Heathrow upon his return from the first Grand Prix of the 1975 season with a running prototype.

'On the Saturday preceding Colin's return there was a severe wheel balance problem. Very decently a local concern cleared off and left us to tackle it alone with our new and still secret prototype!

'I was determined that we should not just drive the car straight down to Heathrow. So Colin Spooner and I spent Sunday grunting round the Hethel test track, putting 250 miles on it before I set out on Monday to meet Colin Chapman.

'I don't think Mr Chapman ever really believed I drove the car down there to meet him. I'm sure he was convinced we'd taken it on a trailer! He was *very* surprised to see a runner, and he did drive it part of the way back. Not all the way, I'm sorry to say. A hub carrier broke, but we had his personal Elite on hand as well, so it wasn't a tragedy.

'We had proved on the Sunday that it all worked, and all worked reasonably well. The steering *was* heavy and—on the way down to London—we proved that it would leave a nosy big Jensen happily for dead!' Rudd remembered that hectic long weekend clearly.

Admitting the failure of the hub carrier prompted the important memory that the original design for the lower rear suspension link to the hub was via a single trailing arm. That was changed immediately afterwards to accommodate the addition of a 'tie-bar' only. There were other rear suspension problems that resulted from the basic concept of simplicity inherent in Lotus

Part of the Lotus in house production facility is this Stuttgart manufactured Trumpf pattern cutting machine. Basically you feed in sheet metal and it cuts out the pattern according to instructions fed in via the computer on the right

philosophy that we shall explore later. The back end was never fully satisfactory until top link was added to do the job that the driveshafts had been undertaking for Series 1, 2, and 2.2.

The prototype had no overheating problems with the radiator mounted in the pod position at the front. In fact, it was quite a problem to get the motor to run warm enough to operate the heater satisfactorily, particularly the demister. Unfortunately production cars were not blessed with such coolness, and a number of modifications had to be made which are detailed in later chapters.

The first running prototype also featured Ate disc brakes, the rear installation of an Alfa Romeo type. Word of the non-power assisted layout got back to Girling, who were reportedly 'not amused'. Originally the British company had not been too interested in the small numbers

Lotus would require, but presumably the prestige of such an association prompted them to take a second look at the situation.

The result was a set of special calipers, but the front disc itself—as well as the entire double arm front suspension minus appropriate dampers, springs and anti-roll bar—was, in the words of Colin Spooner, 'a virtual corner from an Opel Ascona'.

The original show car had one set of large wheels and tyres with hand made Goodyears being carried from display to display. The rears were a massive 265 section—more than the Turbo needed years later! In the opinion of some of the engineers involved at the time the Esprit was 'wildly over-tyred', but this was an essential part of the Giugiaro look. In fact, the cars that reached the public were the result of a quick suspension and tyre conversion performed when it became necessary to switch to smaller 205 section Dunlops. This move was enforced when neither Dunlop nor Goodyear would make such wide and low profile covers as had been exhibited.

Still with constant ventilation problems and with exhaust noise and all the other legislative requirements to be sorted out (mainly at the Motor Industry Research Association proving grounds), the Esprit was ready to step from prototype to production.

Colin Spooner was transferred back to Lotus Cars at Hethel and so was Dennis Jewell, but Rudd remained at Ketteringham to attack the era of ground effect Grand Prix cars, switching to the Lotus 78, winner of four Grand Prix in 1977 and the product of minds like Ralph Bellamy and Martin Ogilvie, as well as the forward thinking of Chapman and Rudd.

Now it was time to see what the public made of the Esprit.

Chapter 3
Series 1:
showtime to reality

From the Silver Car's debut at Turin in November 1972 to the Esprit's first public appearance at the Paris Salon in October 1975, Lotus had been through some of the toughest times in their colourful history. As with the later announcement of the Esprit Turbo, the decision to show at Paris was a sudden one, bringing the first showing forward by a fortnight, but allowing a fitting European debut with the attendant publicity, instead of the planned double launch at Earls Court of the Esprit and its less expensive front-engined derivative the Eclat. The London showing still took place, but obviously didn't create quite the impact of Paris.

The Esprit was thus shown at a time when a receiver had been appointed by Jensen Motors, following Kjell Qvale's withdrawal. This threatened to lose a major customer for the Lotus 16 valve engine. Esprit came at a time when Lotus were still counting the cost of slashing their volume from Elan/Europa days to a spell as a one product (Elite) company. Lotus had made nearly 17,500 Elans and Elan +2s. Now they'd similarly slashed the workforce from 830 employees (in early 1974) to 385, and survived the fuel crisis. Yet

esprit

"The no compromise Lotus for its driver and one selected companion."

STANDARD FITMENTS
Heater, 2 speed wipers with electric wash, heated rear screen, inertia reel seat belts, hazard warning lights, twin fuel tanks, brake servo, reversing lights, 5-speed gearbox with overdrive fifth gear.
Maximum width: 73¼"
Maximum length: 165"
Maximum height 43¾"

For full specification see reverse.

The Lotus Engine

GENERAL SPECIFICATION
Engine: 4 cylinder Lotus 907
Capacity: 1973 cc (120.4 cu.in.)
Bore/Stroke: 95.2/62.9 mm
(3.75/2.72 ins.)
Cooling: Water
Block: Aluminium
Head: Aluminium
Valves: 2 ohc 4 per cylinder
Compression: 8.4:1
Carburettor: Twin Zenith CD 2SE
Bearings: 5 main
Fuel pumps: SU Electrical

How Lotus sold Esprit in the original brochure. The engine shown in the lower picture is of the Zenith Stromberg emission control type, rather than the double choke twin Dellorto European specification

the need to sell the Eclat and the Esprit and get production above the 20–25 Elites a month mark they were then quoting must have been little short of desperate. As Chapman once told me cheerfully, 'about every six years we hit the brink, and it's all a bit touch and go over the edge of a precipice. We're used to surviving here!' It was five years ago when he said that. . . .

At the Paris and London shows of 1975, the Esprit picked up rave reviews, slightly over-shadowed in *Autosport* by the then new fibreglass Ferrari 308GTB, but an undeniable front page draw for *Motoring News*. The red car illustrated on their cover was *not* the second Giugiaro prototype, but a machine for Don McLauchlan to use in his press and public relations role: it was also the car used to illustrate some of the original catalogue. The show car repeated Giugiaro history by going back to silver, but was in that pre-production span of 'about a dozen cars', that Lotus made before the Esprit went into full production in June 1976. Some of these first cars were painted rather than self-coloured.

While *Autosport* contented themselves, thro-ugh John Bolster, with a simple announcement of the salient points, *Motoring News* editor and former Elan owner Michael Cotton had obviously traced Esprit development with care. Under the headline 'Lotus announce the futuristic mid-engine Esprit at the Paris Show', an inside story added to the front page news considerably. Predicted price was, 'just over £4500 including all tax', and it was pointed out that cockpit safety had played a very important part in design with the ingenious (and light!) Z-section alloy beams in the doors and the strength of a marine ply bulkhead between cockpit and engine, plus built-in steel hoop rollover protection.

Reality

When the Esprit S1 went on sale the price was £5844.13. To put that in perspective, a Capri 3000GT(II) was under £2500 in 1975; the TVR

3-litre 3000M was around £3000; Aston Martin's V8 listed for less than £12,000 while Jaguar, where Michael Kimberley had formerly worked, were matching the Esprit's price fairly closely with an XJ6 at £5612. There was still change out of £7500 if you opted for the 12-cylinder engine. More relevantly the Jaguar XJ-S was launched in October 1975 at a UK price of £8900.

Lotus, or more frequently Giugiaro, seemed to get plenty of praise for the lines. Aerodynamically they were quite sound with a drag coefficient of 0.34 credited to the original 'shovel-spoilered' S1. Today the figure is much the same, with an infinitesimal advantage reported for the S2 and a much better front and rear balance recorded on the Turbo, which had added downforce.

From the dimensions one could see why the aerodynamic figure was not more impressive. To be sure, Esprit was low—just under 44 in., the best part of 10 in. lower than many contemporary saloons! Yet it was also wide, 73.25 in. with a 59.5 in. track that would not have disgraced some formula racing cars or a big Jaguar! Overall length was 165 in. with 96 in. of that occupied by the wheelbase. Kerb weight was quoted at under 2000 lb/910 kgs . . . 1980 lb to be precise. It says much for the basic shape that it remains unaltered today, save for detail work.

A look under the Esprit's then self-coloured fibreglass skin (a unique process that continued from the beginning of series production at least until late 1977, self colour was on the verge of a return when this was written), showed how such low weight in a substantial car could be possible.

First of all, the north–south mounted engine and gearbox had alloy casings for all major parts, including the cylinder head and block and the transmission casings themselves. Weight distribution was and continues to be around 40 per cent

Esprit S1 as presented in brochure form with the spoiler coloured to match the paintwork and a plaid interior that looks fit to grace a Scottish ancestral home. Sales pitch was primarily upon the 'many design features proven by a Team (their capital—JW) that designed and built the racing cars which, to date, have won more Formula One Grands Prix than any other motor vehicle manufacturer, and has done so in less time than its principal competitor.'

The Lotus Esprit is Colin Chapman's latest exotic 2 litre, mid-engined, two seat, high performance sports car incorporating many design features proven by a Team that designed and built the racing cars which, to date, have won more Formula One Grands Prix than any other motor vehicle manufacturer and has done so in less time than its principle competitor.

The Esprit design and development programme has included wind tunnel testing at each stage to ensure maximum aerodynamic efficiency and stability. The

Esprit is powered by the highly successful 16 valve 2 litre Lotus 907 engine which has set new standards of efficiency, power out-put and endurance. The five speed gearbox is designed to match the engine torque and vehicle weight, the installation of which follows current Formula One design practice giving optimum weight distribution. The gear change mechanism is both quick and precise.

The Lotus Esprit, the body and interior of which was styled by Europe's leading stylist, Georgetto Giugiaro, is

manufactured utilising the very latest Glass Fibre Reinforced Plastic (G.F.R.P.) technology and incorporates many of the safety features proven in the successful Lotus Elite which, in 1975, was awarded Europe's most coveted safety award, the Don Safety Trophy.

The luxurious interior is upholstered in washable fabric giving maximum comfort, warmth in Winter and coolness in Summer. Fitted head restraints and deep comfortable semi-reclining seats give the driver and

passenger superb comfort and minimum fatigue. Command and information services are grouped within a three panel console, the left hand panel provides lighting control, the central panel provides driving information and the right hand panel houses the environmental controls. The electric window switches are housed in the central tunnel accessible to both driver and passenger. Twin fuel tanks give the Esprit a fuel capacity of 15 gallons and a safe range of approximately 300 miles. A luggage capacity of

[the remainder of lower-left column illegible]

[centre column text illegible]

The secondary safety encompasses the structural design of body and chassis to afford the occupants a wide margin of protection in the event of a collision. The phenomenal impact qualities of glass fibre reinforced plastic (G.F.R.P.) plus the integral "safety cell" structure of the body shell, which three panel set new standards of passenger security.

The Lotus Esprit, breathing STYLE, PERFORMANCE and SAFETY from ENGINE BAY, truly represents TODAY'S Lotus and tomorrow's TOMORROW.

at the front and 60 per cent or so at the back.

The chassis followed Lotus's production practice of the sixties and seventies in having a simple sheet steel box centre section with a very simple 'cradle' to hold the rear engine, and a transverse T-section at the front to lead out to that Ascona front suspension layout. At the back the long Armstrong dampers were surrounded by coil springs and inclined from the aluminium hub to the top steel transverse mounting. This picked up the damper top mounts, and was located both by steel tubes from the main engine frame and by bolts to the fibreglass body.

The rear suspension itself was a model of Chapman thought, in combining comparatively soft damping and springing for a sporting purpose. It also used a very effective box-framed trailing arm and the additional transverse tie-bar that was found necessary after the hub carrier prototype incident. As we have said, the top link was the fixed length driveshaft in effect, a principle that Lotus had successfully used before, but which was to find a limit in a car of this handling ability. The engine had to be modified in the sump baffling to prevent surge at the 0.88g or so that Lotus recorded in hard cornering. 'A figure that we should not really give,' mused Mr Rudd, 'as we find it doesn't co-relate to the figures given by others.' Since there are very few cars in the same cornering league as any Lotus, never mind an Esprit, I felt the Lotus figure was worth publishing.

Front suspension we have already discussed, but it is useful to note that the proprietary rack and pinion steering was not, in itself, responsible for the heavy and rather woolly (by Lotus standards) steering response. Colin Spooner informed me, 'this was the result of the anti-dive measures we took on the front suspension. All I

This brochure was to a similar layout as that of the white car depicted on an earlier page, but the subject vehicle was a red one from the pre-production 1975 run. Inside, the plaid is darker and there are a few minor changes. Here the specification carries the original claims to an overall touring fuel consumption figure of 33 mpg, a maximum speed of 138 mph and 0–60 mph in 6.8 seconds. Even the most favourable magazine tests did not echo such amazing performance/economy balance, but the car was nevertheless well received by most of the media. Incidentally the brochure included engine timing details and even recommended tyre pressures—18 lb front and 28 rear—for the S1

32

esprit

GENERAL SPECIFICATION	Engine: 4 cylinder Lotus 907 Capacity: 1973 cc (120.4 cu in) Bore/stroke: 95.2/62.9 mm (3.75/2.72 in) Cooling: Water Block: Aluminium Head: Aluminium Valves: D ohc 4 per cylinder Valve timing: Inlet opens: 30° btdc Inlet closes: 50° abdc Ex opens: 50° bbdc Ex closes: 30° atdc Compression: 9.5:1 Carburettor: Two Dellorto DHLA 45 Bearings: 5 main Fuel pump: SU Electrical Maximum power: 160 bhp at 6200 rpm Maximum torque: 140 lbs ft at 4900 rpm

Transmission
Type: 5 speed manual
(Clutch: 8½" diaphragm spring hydraulically operated)
Internal ratios and mph/1000 rpm
Fifth 76:1 21.85
Fourth 97:1 17.15
Third 1.32:1 12.58
Second 1.94:1 8.56
First 2.92:1 5.69
Final Drive 4.375:1

Body/Chassis
Construction: GFRP body. Steel backbone/spaceframe chassis (undersealed)

Suspension
Independent unequal length wishbones and coil springs. Telescopic shock absorbers. Torsion bar stabiliser
Camber: 0° to -½°
Alignment: 3 to 5 mm toe-in
Rear: Independent diagonal trailing arm and lateral link with fixed length driveshaft, coil springs, telescopic shock absorbers
Camber: 0° to -½°
Alignment: 8 to 10 mm toe-in

Steering
Type: Rack and pinion
Castor: 3° to 3½°
Kingpin: 9°

Brakes
Type: 9.7 ins disc front/10.6 ins rear (rear inboard)
Circuit: Dual tandem. Split front/rear
Wheels/Tyres 7 J x 14" rear 6 J x 14" front
205/70HR14 195/70HR14
Pressure 28 lbs rear 18 lbs front

Electrical
Polarity: NEG Earth
Alternator: Lucas 18 ACR (45 amp)
Fuses: 4
Headlights: 4 Lucas 5" sealed Beam 75/60 watts

Performance
Maximum speed 138 mph
Speed in gears 1st 41.5
2nd 62.5
3rd 91.8
4th 125.2
O/D 138
(at 6300 rpm)

Acceleration from rest Seconds
0- 30 2.4
0- 40 3.3
0- 50 4.9
0- 60 6.8
0- 70 9.1
0- 80 12.0
0- 90 16.1
0-100 20.7
Maximum 138
Standing ¼ mile 15 seconds

Fuel Consumption
Overall touring: 33 mpg
Tank capacity: 15 gallons
Cruising range: 480 miles

Dimensions
Height 43¾"
Width 73¼"
Length 165
Wheelbase 96
Front track 58
Rear track 59
Ground clearance 5½
Boot capacity 7.0 cu ft
Weight (kerb) 1980 lbs

Lotus

Norwich Norfolk NR14 8EZ Telegrams: Lotus Norwich Telex: 97401 Telephone Wymondham (095 360) 3411

Clean lines of S1 displayed against the functional build of a F86 Volvo truck, a fast way to get the roadgoing Lotus to the customer

can say is that it was originally a lot worse!'

The dual circuit Girling brakes recalled racing history with their use of inboard rear discs. At the time Lotus thought they would save ventilated disc brakes for the V8 model, this initial Esprit keeping solid discs of just under 10 in. diameter front and 10.6 in. rear with no servo assistance.

Throughout the S1 run, Wolferace wheels were used. Lotus had intended to use Speedline wheels of their own design that eventually appeared on the S2. The 14 in. diameter Wolferaces remained, however, as an S1 feature complete with shiny chrome finish. Those on the rear were of 7J section and were one inch wider than those at the front. Although 205/70 HR Dunlops were mentioned as the likely production fitment, most of the cars we saw and tested used a mixture of those

Dunlops at the rear and 195/70 HR Super Sports at the front. The car had however, been previously exhibited on Goodyears, sometimes with their enormous 265/70s at the rear.

Electrics were mainly by Lucas, and included their 18ACR alternator and quadruple 5 in. diameter sealed beam headlamps within the pods. These were raised by a single electric motor with a bulky transfer shaft to the unpowered pod.

Body beautiful: the red original publicity and marketing S1 reveals a line that is still admirable today

The Body

Fundamentally, even in latest guise, the style and simplicity of manufacture of the Esprit body has remained unaltered. When you consider that it was Giugiaro's first encounter with fibreglass

A batch of Eclat bodies go through the unique Lotus body production process for GFRP (Glass Fibre Reinforced Plastic). As with the Eclat/Elite the Esprit body comes down to a separation between top and bottom halves that have to be glued and bolted together. However some early Esprits were manufactured using the self colouring process and Concorde specified paints (presumably the only ones that would stand the fibreglass moulding process?)

when he started work on the Red Car, it is in itself an eloquent testament to Ital Design and the effectiveness of the Lotus management shuttle service to Turin.

The body is constructed in two halves, the top and bottom both glued and bolted to each other in a process that reminds one of a giant modelling kit. All the glass reinforced plastic (GRP) that we discuss in the main body structure is made by the Lotus low pressure injection moulding process: at that time, and for much of the S1 run, such manufacture also included the self-colouring process. Initially this was in just red, white and

Above *Series 2 Esprits coming down the civilized Lotus notion of a production line, with a Series 1 being completed in the foreground. Complete with engine, transmission and suspension, the workers are beginning the trim and electrical installation*

Left *A stage further on as these LHD Series 1 Esprits have their windscreens in place and further interior work carried out*

37

blue because the paints were diamond hard polyurethanes picked up from the Concorde programme! Later a wider range of colours, including the very popular yellow, was available, but the bugbear of the process was its inability to cope with the sparkling metallics that customers in this price bracket demand. Self colouration presented no unusual repair and finish problems, unlike the much-researched pigmented body-work of the 1950s.

The main panels in an Esprit are—top and bottom halves of the main body structure, a large rear hatchback (opened by a release in the door pillar) which hatch Giugiaro incorporated at Lotus's request in place of the larger original of the Red Car, and a conventional bonnet, wherein can be found the spare wheel and, for the resourceful, luggage space. The petrol caps are in fibreglass, as are the twin cant rails to the outside of the roof (one of the moulding modifications). Fibreglass is also used for the two lower sills on

Right *Federal Esprit body receives the drilling and cutting treatment after body panel assembly, ready for final preparation and subsequent mechanical attachments*

Far right *2-litre Type 907 engines being assembled at Hethel. In the foreground the upturned block neatly displays the oil pressure pick up piping and filter while the men further back work on the all alloy cylinder block and the block/head assembly*

either side plus the headlamp pods and the black painted bumpers of the original.

Modifications over the years have concentrated on the front spoiler and a number of Turbo changes to manage the air both inside the body and outside: these are discussed in the appropriate chapters, but suffice it to say in summary that the body proved a great deal more satisfactory than the original chassis!

Chassis details included handling the passage of water via tubing from the Covrad front radiator back to the engine, and the provision of two separate fuel tanks on either side, behind each seat and forward of the back subframe, each holding $7\frac{1}{2}$ Imperial gallons. The engine was installed with its 45° slant, a dead give away to the 90° V8 aspirations of the company and one aspect of the original 907 design that appealed strongly to Mr Chapman. The motor was covered by a simple and crude one-piece cover on sprung clips.

The engine and its transmission were mounted in the chassis by four flexible rubber joints. These played a critical role in the car's character, for, if the engine were mounted with soft rubber bushings, then it could flex and upset the rear wheel angles through the driveshaft top location system. If, on the other hand, the engine were stiffly mounted the resulting Noise, Vibration and Harshness (NVH) problem could be heard and felt!

Performance

The S1 carried a Lotus 907 engine giving 160 bhp at 6200 rpm and 140 lb ft. torque at a high 4900 rpm. Both fourth and top (fifth) gears had ratios below 1:1, providing 17.15 mph per 1000 rpm in fourth and 21.85 mph/1000 rpm in fifth. Lotus

reported theoretical gear speeds of $41\frac{1}{2}$, $62\frac{1}{2}$, 92 and 125 mph in the four lower gears, but based their theory on using 7300 rpm, whereas road testers were normally advised to keep 7000 revs in mind as a maximum.

At 6300 rpm Lotus reckoned the car should be

What the owner does not normally see: the front of Esprit engine showing the three ancillary belt drives from the crankshaft nose, and the cogged belt drive for the two overhead camshafts

41

Preparation and assembly of the 16 valve, four valve per cylinder, Lotus head. The gentleman closest to the camera fettles the head ready for the installation of those two inlet and exhaust valves per cylinder, as performed by the man in the middle

travelling at 138 mph in fifth. They also claimed 15 seconds for the standing $\frac{1}{4}$ mile (very close to 400 metres), 0–60 mph in 6.8s and 0–100 mph in 20.7s. This was allied to an overall mpg figure of 28, which meant an effective range of 400 miles plus!

I was fortunate to have two cracks at the S1. The first impression was abruptly curtailed, but not before I had realised the immense harshness of a pre-production example. A later S1 came my way in July 1977 and had the benefit of additional soundproofing as well as the double-glazed glass interior division between cockpit and engine.

Here it is relevant to note that I covered a standing quarter mile in 16.02s with an S1 and reached 60 mph from rest in 8.28 seconds, with a mean of 26 mpg and a flat road maximum of 130 mph. These findings were largely similar to the fifth wheel figures of *Autocar* upon the same car (RCL 377R).

Inside, the Esprit was a strange mixture of a cheap plastic two spoke steering wheel (the spokes far broader than today) and a very cheering move upmarket in trim and equipment, including electric windows and tartan plaid insets for the fixed back bucket seats.

The Veglia instruments, green with white numerals, included 160 mph speedometer and 7000 rpm redlined tachometer of matching diameter. Smaller circular dials recorded oil pressure, water temperature, battery voltage condition and fuel contents. All the dials were vaguely marked and the fuel gauge particularly disliked coping with inter-connected tanks on either side of a hard cornering car!

Air conditioning was not part of the original specification, but was introduced by Lotus using much of their own equipment together with a General Motors AC Delco compressor. The company had already discovered that one electric fan was not enough at the front, but when the AC was specified, with its additional gills in front of the main radiator, three fans were needed!

Internally the handbrake would always catch you out on an Esprit with its right-hand location near the door sill in RHD cars, but the gearchange worked as well as promised. Colin Spooner recalled, 'super gearchange on those early cars: in fact I think they were the best. Since then we've compromised a little, but immediately after the Europa our priority was to get the change right.' Tony Rudd echoed the thought behind their work in 1976, 'you pay £7000 odd for the gearchange and the rest is free', he told Denis Jenkinson and me before my first encounter with the Esprit!

Also at the tail end of 1976 Mr Rudd expanded on why it had taken so long to get S1 into genuine series production: 'I reckon we solved 90 per cent of the problems before manufacture, but there were others who reckoned I solved 10 per cent and they did the rest trying to put it into production!'

Certainly from the Easter 1975 delivery of the running prototype to full production some fifteen months later took more time than the 'stick-the-plans-in-the-boot-and-we'll-make-it' attitude they had hoped for, but life never has been easy for the small specialist.

By the time I drove the car in the summer of 1977 the price reflected both those earlier delays and savage inflation, for it had already reached £8548 and the £10,000 Esprit was in sight. When that psychological barrier was reached Lotus would have to offer more than just eye catching looks and (whatever mistakes they made) amazing handling.

Ventilation, of both cockpit and engine bay were priorities, as were more creature comforts and the shovelling of as much air as possible through that front radiator. Detail work during the S1 run had helped things like the sealing and fit of the rear hatch; the durability of the exhaust system and the catches for the tailgate.

After producing 994 cars between June 1976 and May 1978 it was time for the S2. Incidentally, the original S1 was exported in 130 bhp twin Stromberg carburettor emission trim to the USA from 1 January 1977.

Chapter 4
Series 2: cosmetic progress

Around a thousand customers purchased the Series I Esprit. Now it was time to incorporate some of their comments, and those of the press, in the specification of second series (S2). The fundamental problems of rear suspension and chassis strength would remain in the pending file for a while longer. Thus the S2 looked a lot better and was sharply improved in respect of cockpit creature comforts, but was fundamentally the same motor car.

There was one important mechanical change that affected all Lotus 16-valve engines made from late in the S1 run in 1977, and descended from comments made by customers in the early days of the Elites. Tony Rudd tells the story of the E (for Emission) camshaft development. 'We were getting a feedback from Elite customers early on that they would forgo the 6000 rpm plus performance levels in exchange for a bit more mid-range pull, effectively between 70–90 mph on a 3.7 axle.'

The Lotus answer was also to provide better emission level readings in the lab Lotus have operated since 1974. Incidentally, that emission laboratory is one of very few in Britain (six, Lotus reckon) and a rarity in that Lotus can run their own emission certification programmes, including the 50,000 mile requirement, around their own Hethel track, and have the results accepted by the Environmental Protection Agency in the USA. By the early eighties Lotus were still selling in America and Japan, not the full range but most of the non-turbo models. They had also met the differing Australian standards with everything but the Turbo, and were thus better placed than any British manufacturers in respect of emission knowledge and readiness for the tightening laws of Europe that looked set to cause major problems for some larger UK-based manufacturers.

So, the later Esprit S1 and all subsequent S2s enjoyed an engine with notable pulling power between three and five thousand rpm, but which still revved to 7000 in the gears, if required. The

Below Jon O. Atkinson's cutaway drawing shows the Esprit in S2 trim with appropriate wheels, remote control door mirror and revised fascia. It also reveals that rear suspension design for S1 to S2.2 with considerable clarity, as well as the disposition of the major components like the front mounted radiator and north-south mid engine/transmission layout

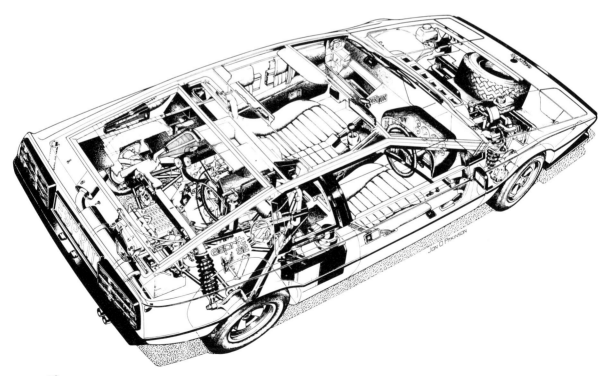

result was a small mpg bonus too, owing to the reduced gearchanging needs of the torquier E-cam unit.

Externally the S2 offered some noticeable changes. The wheels were the result of a long gestation period and the design work of Lotus coupled to the production facilities of Speedline in Italy, a Lotus Grand Prix wheel supplier. Much the same sporting link would later exist between Lotus and Goodyear for the Esprit Turbo.

The Speedline wheels were of cast alloy four spoke design and offered the practical benefit of an extra inch in track, measuring seven inches across the front rims and $7\frac{1}{2}$ in. at the back. Originally the Wolferace wheels were only intended as a brief stop gap on the introduction of the S1, but they survived the model's run, the Speedlines not being ready until 1978 and the S2.

Externally the biggest changes for S2 were the Anglo-Italian wheel design, a new wrap around front spoiler, badgework and redesigned door mirrors

Tyre sizes were unchanged officially, but I note from my former *Motor Sport* colleagues that Dunlop 205 VR Supersports were on the test S2 they had in March 1979, S2 with a 60 per cent low profile front and 70 per cent rear. The spare was then a 13 in. Speedline with a 185/70 VR as a 'get-you-home' spare.

Aerodynamically speaking, Mike Kimberley recalled this as the best body, but it was just a matter of fractions. The S2 was recalled as having a coefficient of 0.335, the slight improvement due to typical Lotus air management modifications. First there was the full width, wrap-around front spoiler. This not only helped inherent stability compared to the original, but also shovelled air more effectively at the S2's enlarged radiator.

The second aerodynamic change was the adoption of 'ears'. The most effective was behind the nearside rear window. It scooped air into the frequently heated rear luggage compartment and also helped reduce condensation on the rear screen in high humidity conditions. This early form of internal air ducting included a direct supply of cold air to the carburettors. At the time Lotus said (in a release that also recorded the manufacture of an extra 400 or so Esprits than history has shown to be the case!) 'A further benefit from the cold air ram feed is to improve volumetric efficiency, giving 0–60 mph acceleration time improvements from 7.1s to 6.8s and 0–100 from 20.2s to 19.4s.'

You will observe there is a matching 'ear' on the offside of the S2 Esprit. This simply feeds cold air to the engine area, where it was useful in cooling the hard worked twin cam.

Other external changes included the ridged Rover 3500 tail lights with their vacuum-moulded ABS plastic surrounds in matt black, just one of many vacuum mouldings the company use. One

Top right S2 displays its new wheels and front spoiler to advantage. It seems this may well have been the most aerodynamically efficient Esprit of all

Lower right The RHD and LHD (furthest away) Esprit pose on the Hethel runways in S2 guise. Note the use of side flashing indicators and yet bigger bumpers on white North American-bound Esprit

practical benefit of the new rear lamps was the installation of high intensity fog warning lights.

Aside from the new front spoiler, 'ears' and the revised rear lamps, the S2 also looked different in the showroom because of the matt black chip-resistant paint treatment adopted for the new spoiler, sills and rear valance, plus the double coachline strip carrying S2 decals on the three-quarter panel. This was close up to the point where the original car simply said esprit in lower case lettering.

Internally better . . .

One very important change in the cause of visibility was the use of twin electric motors to power the lifters for the headlamps, now of $5\frac{1}{2}$ in. halogen type.

The instrumentation always was comprehensive, but the vague Veglia dials gave way on S2 to simple and legible Smiths black and white

Revised S2 interior with slider switchgear and revised instrumentation shows off optional leather seating and part trim. The rather clumsy steering wheel remained until the advent of Turbo and S3

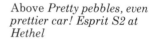

Above *Pretty pebbles, even prettier car! Esprit S2 at Hethel*

Left *New Rover sourced tailights are prominently displayed, together with S2 number plate frame (vacuum formed, like the bumpers, within Lotus factory) while this S2 gets the low speed handling treatment. It looks hardworked enough to be a works development hack!*

S2 Esprit body is lowered down over the chassis and running gear. Note the way the exhaust runs across the back section

instruments. As before speed (to 160 mph) and engine rpm (to a maximum 8000 rpm) were the major dials in front of the driver. Oil pressure, battery volts, fuel tanks content and water temperature were now more accurately calibrated than before.

The number of warning lights was increased, including one for electric fan failure, very important in an alloy-headed mid-engine vehicle! Paddle slide switches replaced the original rocker action switchgear, and illumination was reportedly a lot better with the fibre optics system, still used today. The electric window switches were moved from their original position on top of the gear lever tunnel down to face the back of the gear lever.

The S2 trim was massively improved especially with a £200 plus Connolly leather option for the seats. Even if you did not take that option, the car looked more fashionable inside, thanks to a kind of suedette finish applied to the previously bald instrument binnacle. The same material went all over the fascia flat panels, front screen pillars, and part of the door trims. The seats were recontoured, allowing an inch extra headroom according to Lotus, and an extra two inches width through wider cushions.

If that detail were not enough for you, there was always the digital clock as an internal identification.

Some important changes took place around the engine. The Meccano kit with springs that Lotus offered as an engine cover on the S1 was dispensed with in favour of a cover having an inspection hatch let into the fibreglass to allow faster checks on oil and water levels. Changing spark plugs in this mid-engined device was not a task for the chicken hearted: a slant mid engine was not an encouragement to the DIY man, but then neither was the traditional Lotus home for the distributor, underneath the Dell'Ortos. This weak link was only convincingly improved by breakerless ignition systems, used on 2.2 engines.

Detail on the S2 rear light cluster of Rover 3500 origin. Henceforth rear fog warning lights were incorporated besides the ridged glass with matt black surround

LHD North American S2 also had the Giugiaro styling badge on the O/S panel, bigger bumpers and revised front indicator arrangments

Also new on the S2 was an intermediate silencer for the exhaust system, plus aluminium finish for downpipes and 'aluminised steel silencer and tail pipes'. Lotus engineers simply remember that they spent plenty of time fiddling around with the exhaust as a whole, throughout the life of the car. . . .

Pricing: up, up and away!

When the S2 was announced the price was £11,124.37. By the time Clive Richardson tried it for *Motor Sport* the tag read £11,754, or around

£12,000 with leather upholstery. When it went out of production in December 1979—but remember there were S2s available in UK stock well into 1980—the Esprit was priced at either £14,175 or £14,870, this when Lotus were heavily involved in a programme of offering alternative levels of equipment as separate packages (eg: Elite 501, 502, 503 and 504, the latter primarily denoting an automatic).

Thus, from a design price of 'around £4500' to an announcement price in the £5800 bracket Lotus had taken the Esprit up roughly three times in price! It was a lot to ask, even if *Motor* did acknowledge a maximum speed of 130 mph. Slightly down on the factory test results of 138 mph. The magazines tended to disagree with the Lotus claim of 0–60 mph in 6.8s too. *Motor* got 7.7s for their Lotus demonstrator and reported an overall 19 mpg, though they did report a touring fuel consumption of 26 mpg.

From June 1978 to January 1980 some 980 Esprit S2s were made, 100 of these from the individually numbered Limited edition for the UK. These were launched to celebrate Lotus's victory in the 1978 Constructors World Championship. The special S2s offered the tradi-

Worn with justifiable pride, the Lotus record as a manufacturer in Grand Prix racing. It could do with an eighties' title to go along with the other two decades of solid success . . .

Celebrating their domination of the 1978 World Championship (Lotus won the constructor's title and Ronnie Peterson was runner-up to World Champion driver Mario Andretti), Lotus produced an individually numbered S2 Esprit special edition. The external numbering can be seen on this 001 example where the Esprit badge would normally be carried

tional JPS black and gold coachlined paintwork plus a sporting steering wheel (the standard S1 and S2 wheel was a rather unhappy object that would have been far more at home in a safety-conscious saloon of the seventies), radio/cassette deck and a commemorative plaque. It was this win that brought Lotus up to seven Grand Prix World Championship titles in the Constructors section of the Championship, so there was quite a lot to get onto that plaque!

As to the S2 itself, I had minimal first hand experience. I do know some gentlemen now in their thirties who owned S2s from brand new and can confirm that their memories tended to be dominated by the troubles they had, and they tend to have Porsche 911s today!

. . . But that is not the whole story. When he heard I was writing this book, one of those former Lotus customers said to me, 'the Esprit is such a

lovely looking car. I remember mine this way: when it was going, it was the most beautiful car in the world. A dream! What used to get me down were the details, just niggly little things, and then the Porsche was about the same money. Now that Lotus are more realistically priced again and there's that Turbo, yeah I might have an Esprit again. I mean it was a *luvverly* looking motor!'

Another S2 customer remembered the headlamps nearly sending him blind with their wavering up and down when extended, but I think Mr Richardson put it best in *Motor Sport*: '... Yet at the end of the day there aren't many cars around so enjoyable to drive as this latest mid-engine Lotus. I would love to have one in my garage if somebody else's money bought it.'

They were going the right way, but something else was needed to stay competitive in this price bracket....

Threequarter front, the black and gold Esprit—its colour scheme reflecting John Player Special (JPS) livery—displays the side strip proclaiming the 1978 World Championship as well as the garland that went around the Lotus bonnet badge, plus the rear quarter deck limited edition number

Chapter 5
Turbocharged revival: engine

It was February 12, 1980. Everything about the launch of the Esprit Turbo was in the best show business traditions. Since the car went on to become a Bond film star, such a launch was not in such bad taste as those who hadn't been invited (myself included) felt at the time. The important point for the Esprit aficionado was that the car was a genuine turning point in Esprit and Lotus fortunes—and it was a much better all round car, not just a 150 mph headline-grabber.

The first turbocharged car from Lotus was the star of a multi thousand pound evening, sponsored by Essex Petroleum at the Royal Albert Hall with Shirley Bassey (who reputedly cost a little more than the initial £21,000 charged for the Essex Esprit Turbo originally!). Amidst the extravagant Essex trappings of food for 700 guests supplied by the Dorchester Hotel, the 210 bhp blue, silver and red Esprit (one of three then in existence!) certainly performed its publicity role immaculately. What caught the headlines, of course, was the emotive 150 mph claim, in fact justified by a tougher testing programme than any previous Lotus had endured. When the press came to drive the car a few months later, it was found that the chassis was just as remarkable as that flexible and simple turbocharger layout. How Lotus achieved such docility and set the tone for ordinary Esprits of the following year is a worthy tale.

The missing eight

As Tony Rudd confessed to me in 1982, 'really the car that turned out to be the Essex Turbo could have been the M71 Esprit V8. Look at the chassis 'cradle' for the engine; you'll see it's got space for another bank of exhausts. Nobody comments on that, but I promise you that's what the extra space is for. The idea of slotting another cylinder bank onto the slant four has always appealed to Colin.'

Ardent supporter and then manager of the Turbo project was Powertrain Engineering Manager Graham Atkin. Graham was responsible for all detail engineering as well as management and deserves his place in Lotus history, for he had to argue the Turbo project through against more senior Lotus executives who favoured the V8. The Esprit Turbo was his last Lotus project for he left, 'covered in glory', in late 1979 for a post as Chief Engineer at Austin Rover Advanced Engines.

To understand the Turbo's 2.2 litre engine fully it is important to discuss the Lotus 16-valve engine in greater depth. The basic unit we see today, a slant four with die cast alloy block, wet cylinder liners, and alloy head containing 16 valves and two overhead camshafts, dates back to Chapman's expressed 1965–66 desire for an engine of his own. This would replace the Twin Cam they built in association with Ford—a unit that had too many components outside Chapman's control for comfort, and in which Ford had lost interest.

Rudd remembers that a few leading figures were asked to make their suggestions around this period. His answer was a 120° V6 utilising the

Twin Cam Lotus heads. That was too wide to fit in Elan. By 1967/68 ex-Coventry Climax designer Ron Burr was drawing up a slant four with 16 valve layout that appealed strongly to Chapman for its possible Indy use as a doubled-up V8.

Rather unfortunately, Chapman saw the Vauxhall slant four iron-block engine. At the time he was very worried about the enormous costs of putting his own die-cast alloy motor into production. The Vauxhall link was a useful short cut to mount the Lotus 16-valve head and prove it in action, this including the racing LV 220 motors that featured on the Lotus 62 sports racers driven by Messrs Muir and Miles in the late sixties in Gold Leaf colours. Yet the link with Vauxhall is one that is regretted today by some Lotus senior management as confusing the present engine's pure Lotus manufacture.

Tony Rudd arrived at Lotus from BRM in September 1969 'to turn Lotus into an engine manufacturer'.

For eight months of 1969 and the opening third of 1970 Rudd prepared the engine for production, buying the machinery to create the 2-litre, die-cast alloy, motor. Amongst those production preparations was a slimming course for the cylinder block which brought machining time down from $1\frac{1}{2}$ hours to 55 minutes. This was achieved mainly by removing ancillaries like pumps from integral block construction to separate manufacture.

Ron Burr went to Jaguar, where he was still a successful engine man when this was written, while prototype testing of some 14 prototype Lotus engines, with sand cast alloy cylinder blocks, went ahead. Many of the running prototype engines were installed in Vauxhalls, further confusing the engine's parentage.

The basic combustion chamber owed a lot to

Left *Its front drive belts
modestly, and safely,
shrouded, this is the Lotus
Type 912 engine at home in
the then Chrysler Sunbeam
Lotus. The 2.2 litre stretch
was first seen in the Chrysler
and amounted to much
strengthened engine along
the original 2 litre Type 907
16 valve principles*

Below *The high performance
Chrysler, which was later
sold as a Talbot. Lotus also
developed the suspension and
braking*

Lotus unveil the Type 910 which combines an exhaust driven turbocharger, pressure feeding the Dell'Orto carburettors, and the 2.2 litre DOHC with the original 16 valves. Complete with 7.5:1 cr and 8 lb boost the engine developed 210 bhp at 6250 rpm and 200 lb ft torque. Put another way, it was at least 70 bhp more than the original Type 907!

high speed racing techniques, and the company still feel that such knowledge has helped them enormously in meeting the varied world standards of exhaust emissions.

When Donald Healey and Kjell Qvale took over Jensen in 1970, one of their earliest moves was to search out an engine supplier for their projected sports car. As Rudd put it so aptly, 'they were searching for an engine, we were searching for a customer'. The reason Lotus were looking for customers for an engine which they knew they would use themselves one day, was simply to get an economic cost per engine produced on the sophisticated machinery acquired to make this advanced four.

These would go into Jensen Healeys made from 1972 to 1976: in addition, from 1975, there was also the similarly-powered Jensen GT coupé. In Jensen form, Lotus quoted 140 bhp at 6500 rpm and 130 lb ft. torque on 5000 revs.

It was this that boosted the Lotus engine so sharply, though it has to be remembered they also did 'a nice little deal', with Chrysler and their successors Talbot to supply a stretched 2.2 litre version of that engine (Type 912). Instead of 1973 cc (95.2 mm by 62.9 mm bore and stroke) there was the same bore stroked by a 76.2 mm crankshaft, ironically a crankshaft throw from Vauxhall's stretch of their iron block slant four to 2.3 litres.

This 2.2 litre capacity was to be important to Lotus, since it formed the base of both the Turbo motor and of a subsequent normally aspirated engine for Hethel at that original stretch size of 2172 cc.

The original plan was to produce 10,000 Lotus 16-valve engines a year, some 5000 of them for Jensen. Running flat out Lotus did eventually manage to hit a rate equivalent to 7500 pa, but the problem was always to synchronize production rates with Jensen.

In principle, Rudd looks back on the Lotus four cylinder's record with pride, for it has not been fundamentally changed since going into production, save for the increase in capacity and the engineering associated with turbocharging. The

Inside the Essex first edition of the Turbo Esprit was the bulbous leather finish for the seating, plus a roof mounted FM only radio with cassette player at the front. The two spoke wheel was of a more sporting design and air conditioning was a standard feature of these Essex-emblazoned models

New engine and chassis: the turbocharged engine at home in the rear of the revised chassis, which importantly featured a top link to take the rear suspension loads. Temperature control within the engine bay was a primary development objective

principles are still the same but the details have been altered to beat production problems. The prototype sand-cast engines ran beautifully, but when the die-cast motors became production reality, it was found that the oil would not drain back from the cam box area, especially if more than 6000 rpm were used.

'Long term, the answer to that one was a new design of camshaft area drainage and a synthetic oil seal for the crankshaft instead of the rope type we were using,' Rudd revealed.

There were also extreme problems during the 1973/74 miners' strike, when power cuts kept upsetting the delicate electronic tooling, which tended to run amok when the electricity supply surged!

Above *The historic 'Red Car'
registered IDGG 01 was the
working prototype during
1972 and 1973. It wasn't
named 'Esprit' until well into
its testing programme.
Giugiaro and Chapman had
it right from the outset*

*The other 'Silver Car' at the
Earls Court Motor Show in
London in late 1975. The
Paris Show saw the launch a
little earlier that year to rave
reviews. Of course, everyone
knew something of what was
to come*

Opposite page *The S1 in all its glory outside the Lotus factory, on the test track. The Wolfrace wheels help to accentuate the stark simplicity of the design*

Above *The S2 at a similar spot on the factory test track in late 1978. Compared to the S1 the Speedline wheels, coachlines and black sill panel modernize but complicate the appearance*

Left *The major improvement for the S2.2 was obviously the enlarged engine. The 2.2 litre engined peaked 160 bhp but top speed remained at 138 mph. The S2 painting remains but the badging becomes more aggressive*

Left *Quite obvious is the Turbo influence on the S3 photographed in 1982. Everyone loves the BBS wheels and the black detailing. The badges have changed again and there's the new side vent by the lockable fuel filler. The bumpers are wraparound and the Rover tail lamps deeper*

Above *The Turbo interior is manifestly 'luxury'—leather hide just everywhere. Clever roof pod and instrument binnacle persuade the driver to think he's flying even when standing still*

Left *Perhaps the car which
has at last elevated the Lotus
road car into a position to
challenge Ferrari. The Turbo
Esprit can give the 308GTBi
more than a good run for its
money both in terms of speed
and build quality*

Above *A later car (1981
model) than that shown in
the previous photograph,
surprisingly doesn't tell the
driver who has just been
passed what's overtaken him.
Rearwards vision is severely
restricted on this Turbo*

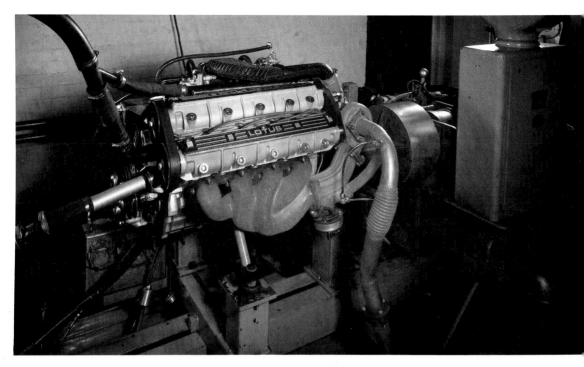

Below *On the test bed heat and noise are generated. This Type 910 engine will produce over 200 horsepower symbolizing Lotus's capability as an engine manufacturer. It's a long way from North London*

Above *Black readily accentuates the large tail spoiler, sill located NACA duct and the car's lowness. Further aerodynamic aids are fitted to the Turbo—lip on the roof just above the rear window and raised edge down the sides of the front screen. 150 mph is available*

When the Elite was launched in 1974, it had a 9.5:1 cr as the most notable change over the Jensen specification (8.4:1), and was claimed to give 155 bhp at 6500 rpm and 135 lb ft. torque, the peak at 5000 revs. Twin Dell'Orto carburettors have been part of the basic Lotus engine specification from the start, except where export emission considerations forced them to twin Zenith-Strombergs and ancillary modifications that left even Hethel claiming only 130 bhp or so at one stage. For S2 in USA they claimed 140 bhp at 5800 rpm and 130 lb ft. torque at 4000 rpm.

With the opening of their emissions laboratory and the need to get the range of newer, upmarket Lotii into every possible market, much of the work on the motor through the seventies concentrated on this vital factor. Certification was sought for places as differing in their demands as Europe, Japan, America and Australia and was achieved. As noted, the E-camshaft, which made the motor much more flexible in town use in original 1973 cc guise, was adopted in 1977.

When the proposition to go for 2.2 litres came up, prompted by Chrysler enquiries and an original estimate for 4500 such cars Rudd was against the idea. He said frankly, 'I thought we'd end up with an engine where the pistons stayed put and the engine went up and down!'

The gist of Rudd's objection lay in the increased vibration that would result from the increase in stroke. In fact this was a major problem. Its answer—'which was not particularly original, I learned it from Rolls before the war', said Rudd with his usual directness—was a very thin disc, or 'flexible flywheel', as it is commonly known inside the company. Thus the engine virtually has a disc with the starter ring gear around it, rather than a conventional flywheel.

For the 2.2 Sunbeam application Lotus had to

Chassis now shared by S3 and Turbo accommodates Elite/Eclat Lotus fabricated front suspension, top link for rear suspension and an engine 'cradle' that can take either V8 or Lotus four cylinder engines

It all goes in there and comes out here! Lotus explanation of their Garrett AiResearch turbocharged layout for the Type 910. Biggest development problems concerned the efficient operation of wastegate pressure release and sustaining piston life on deceleration from high speed. The Dell'Orto carburettors with their pressure-resistant gaskets and other turbocharging tweaks have been gratefully adopted by other turbocharger conversion specialists

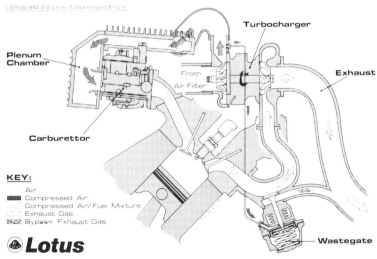

LOTUS 910. 2.2 Litre. Turbocharged Engine

Turbocharger

Plenum Chamber

Exhaust

From Air Filter

Carburettor

KEY:
Air
Compressed Air
Compressed Air/Fuel Mixture
Exhaust Gas
Bypass Exhaust Gas

Wastegate

Lotus

make a new sump to fit the saloon, strengthen the main bearing panels against the increased loads, and thus provide a much stiffer—and unique—bottom end for the motor, which was dubbed the 912 unit in Lotus terminology. Tuned for torque rather than power the Talbot version had a claimed 155 bhp at 5750 rpm and a generous 150 lb ft. at 4500 revs. In rally trim, still tractable enough for occasional road use and fitted with oversize twin choke Webers (48 mm) those Talbot Sunbeam Lotus's were capable of some 240 bhp, and 182 lb ft. torque, enough to win the 1980 RAC Rally and the 1981 World Championship for Talbot. Incidentally Lotus also developed the Talbot Sunbeam road-car suspension and some ancillaries in much the same way as they used some of their Lotus Esprit Turbo suspension principles on the rear engined De Lorean.

Sturdy cast iron exhaust manifolding leads to black and silver T3 turbocharger, the black-cased vanes transferring momentum via a shaft to the silver pressurising section of the unit. The latter feeds the 35 mm choke carburettors via a long and carefully sectioned induction pipe, which also has the task of ensuring mixture temperature stability in the absence of an intercooler

Grrr! Side view of Essex series is cluttered by enough badges to keep any collector happy. The point is the amount of unique aerodynamic and styling features incorporated in Esprit Turbo, a hint of skirted formula car very much the theme of those lower sills. The big rear spoiler is a complete add-on back section to the main body, while the small NACA ducts in front of the rear wheels are part of the air movement system for the engine bay

Esprit technology

As has been explained, the Esprit's original 2-litre 907 engine called for a revised lubrication system to cope with the higher cornering demands. Rudd feels it is probable that the Turbo engine could have lived on in wet sump form, but they opted for a full dry sump system 'for the long distances and high speeds that are possible with Turbo. Quite honestly it's not necessary to dry sump unless you are really thrashing the motor. It grieves me to see the oil cooler virtually bulging on a dry sump system when it's being started from cold!'

The next basic step in a $1\frac{1}{2}$ year engine modification programme which 'took longer than we thought', in Rudd's words, was that the 2.2 litre capacity, as given earlier, would be used . . . but the engine would be *very* different to the one supplied in non-Turbo form to Talbot.

Right up to 1979 Lotus had the M71 project for a

more aggressive Esprit with V8 power running alongside the Turbo programme, but when the decision was taken to go Turbo detail development was rapid. The Turbo motor was chosen primarily on cost grounds one suspects, for even this installation, effective as it is, lacks some items that Lotus engineering might otherwise have incorporated. Fuel injection? An inter-cooler? Microchip-controlled electronic ignition and engine management? All were mentioned and are possible for the future.

Throttle lag and poor low speed torque were avowed primary targets tackled with the in-stallation of a Garrett T3 AiResearch turbo charger to pressurise modified double Dell'Orto 40 DHLA carburettors. The smaller choke Dell'Ortos were modified in that they were calibrated to cope with the varying mixture densities of boost to a final wastegate-controlled maximum of 8lb above atmosphere. The Dell'

Ortos were also fitted with special gaskets and seals to resist leakage under pressure and performed extremely well in action, even allowing a degree of cooling effect. Measured temperature drop at full boost of the intake charge was 40°C by the time it had passed from the turbo and through the carburettor venturi.

Initially Lotus tried downdraught carburation to get the shortest possible inlet tracts, and thus cut response lag. They went back to sidedraught when this didn't work in practice. The delivery pipe from turbine to carburettors was found to be critical in this search for snappy throttle response, and pipe variation in shape from round to oval is the deliberate result of development in this connection. In fact Lotus found the variables they tried altered peak power by up to 25 bhp, and maximum torque reading by 20–25 lb ft.

Perhaps the key to their development hassles was that of compression. The final figure was 7.5:1 instead of 9.5:1 of normal Esprit. This meant they lost 'virtually half the top of the piston' in Rudd's words. Thus it was not surprising that they ran into piston crown melting problems when they began high speed running at the Nardo track in Italy.

A redesigned forged piston (with the skirts reshaped and rings lowered) in conjunction with enlarged cylinder head water flow passages, and a bigger water pump, helped. The combustion chambers received sodium-filled exhaust valves running in Hidural 5 guides. The actual valve seating was hardened, too, and the net effect was a reduction in exhaust valve face temperatures of 100°C.

Temperatures within the mid-engine bay were naturally a matter for concern anyway, with a turbine whipping round at a maximum 110,000 rpm. Then there was the exhaust, high tech and high content silicone-molybdenum iron though it was. A contributory answer was the Lotus use of NACA ducts later in the development programme to feed air from the exterior of the lower sills and up over the engine itself.

Camshafts featured increased lift, from 0.358 in. to 0.380 in. and subtly different timing. For the Turbo the 28 degrees BTDC of the inlets opening was retained from the normal E-camming as was the 28 degrees closure of the exhaust valves (ATDC) but 58 degrees was substituted for the closing of the inlets and opening of the exhausts on Turbo, while the normal Lotus engine used 52 degrees at these points.

Aside from the dry sumping precautions the inherent engine strength was upped sharply. The process is summed up by saying that virtually only the cylinder block and connecting rods were as for the 2.2, though of course most changes were modifications rather than changes in the 16-valve, die-cast alloy, principles that have always ruled this motor.

Is this little devil a Talbot master plan to startle the rally world with a Group B turbocharged version of their rally car? Taken during the 1982 winter, the Talbot was believed to use a mid-mounted and turbocharged version of their Lotus 16 valve engine. Note the fabricated rear suspension and the fact that this prototype is based on the Talbot Horizon, which is normally a front drive hatchback

Chapter 6
Turbo:
body and chassis

Externally, the Turbo Esprit looked different with its deep wrap-round spoiler matched by the NACA-ducted side sills (hinting at single seater racing practice) and the new tail section, which included a rear spoiler and an under-bumper valance housing the exhaust system. In detail it also differed from Esprit in the tiny lip above the rear window and the use of slats. Fundamentally the body of the £21,000 Essex Esprit Turbo and the later, and much cheaper (from £16,982.23) Turbo Esprit were the same, it was just the luxury equipment, decoration and decals that were different. The same applies mechanically too, though the Essex Esprits came fully equipped with items like leather upholstery, air conditioning and the absurdly expensive, FM-only, roof radio that Lotus cut out of the cheaper models. The latter, lacking the emblazoned Essex symbols and mandatory blue, red and silver paint scheme of their 104 Essex edition run, could be specified back up to £20,000 or so by adding all the Essex equipment.

The GRP body had an aerodynamic coefficient of 0.342 in Turbo guise, but was much better balanced aerodynamically front to rear with that tail dam and detail work.

Once again the more aggressive style was the work of Giugiaro (as was the interior) and once more it was modified in the light of wind tunnel and practical experience. The original prototype did not have the NACA ducts in the lower sills, or the lip just in front of the rear window. Neither did it have the full width undertray that made it possible for Lotus to reduce the front end lift of the Giugiaro prototype from 56 lb to 29 lb (the S2 figure was 58 lb) and the rear lift from Giugiaro's original big spoiler configuration −1 (which led to a nose-up speedboat attitude!) to 26 lb, half the rear end lift figure of an S2.

Incidentally the front spoiler was made slightly smaller than the Giugiaro prototype's while they were fighting that rear excess of downforce. Even when I drove the Essex Turbo with chief Lotus test driver Roger Becker in June 1980, the deep front spoiler scraped the ground all too freq-

Price cutter: minus air conditioning and other standard Essex features, the turbo esprit (as Lotus describe the car on the side badging) saved the best part of £4000 when it was launched, early in 1981. As the public recognized the worth of the car so prices crept back up, many specifying the options that had been deleted as part of the price reduction

Above *Slatted engine cover is held down at the front by quick action butterfly nuts. Neat baggage cover hides stowage sufficient, together with front section, for weekend luggage. Baggage will be warm rather than toasted over a long trip*

Above right *Quadruple Hella quartz headlamps and the twin motor raise and lower mechanism provide stable white light that is difficult to imagine for the S1 owner*

uently. This tendency has only been minimised with a slight rise in ride height for the springs.

Pleased though Lotus were with the body, it was the new chassis for Turbo's postponed V8 that made the biggest single contribution to the car's feeling of integral strength. A new front box section allowed the installation of Elite/Eclat upper wishbone and single transverse link front suspension, of pure Lotus design and fabrication.

Torsional rigidity of the new chassis was said to be up by 50 per cent, its frequent use of box and triangulated sheet metal especially noticeable when compared to the original. Also new was the tubular cradle for the engine and transmission (the latter unaltered save for a $9\frac{1}{2}$ in. diameter clutch plate). The chassis was the result of the R&D 'torture rig' Lotus had been able to install in the wake of their De Lorean engineering work.

You could say the vital link was in the rear springing. 'At long last we had to admit defeat over our "minimum components" policy in respect of the rear suspension,' sighed Colin Spooner, a touch wistfully. 'In principle, the fixed length driveshaft acting as the upper link was right along The Chairman's correct principles of

simplicity. Yet, in this case the compromise between fixing rear suspension geometry, and compliance to help engine NVH, simply had to go.'

Tony Rudd added, 'we had always intended to do something about improving the Esprit chassis. When we put together a welded-up Turbo conversion with 200 bhp, we realised there were all sorts of things we now *had* to do, especially with the intended 235 section tyres on the back in a suspension that was originally designed for 185s on an Elite!'

A short top link was installed to take the loads the driveshafts had been accommodating. These shafts were now of the plunging type to accommodate the new geometry.

'The original S1 and S2 chassis design and rear suspension always struck me as a series of disjointed parts. It initially lacked the usual Lotus integrity, in a word,' one Lotus executive told me with stunning frankness. Now that problem was over, for the Turbos at least, as the new chassis and rear suspension immediately imparted a feeling of security and body strength. This was partly because a new four point engine mounting could

Above Massive rear Goodyear NCTs are now optionally available on S3, but lower sills are unique to turbocharged Esprits

Above left Engine cover completely removed one can see that the air shifting layout within the engine bay really works, depositing road grime while keeping the turbocharged four remarkably cool

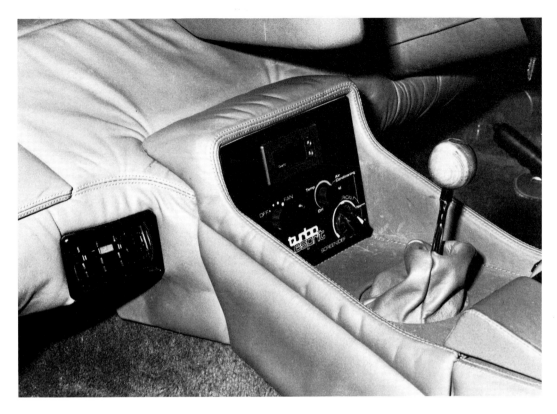

Turbo detail shows fancy leatherwork finish and the air conditioning layout that is so welcome behind that large front screen, even in European spring sunshine

be used which did allow maximum NVH absorbence, for no longer had the motor to be rigidly mounted with the top links doing the work that the driveshafts had previously been asked to cope with.

In two key detail areas Lotus not only disagreed with current practice, but proved they could do a better job. The first surprise was that they did not adopt ventilated disc brakes. The disc size went up for Turbo, with $10\frac{1}{2}$-in. diameter front units, as compared to the original 9.7 in., while the back units were fractionally larger at 10.8 in. instead of the original 10.6 in., this owing more to supplier changes than engineering, for there was no official increase at the rear, and some S2 specifi-

cation sheets still speak of 10.8 in.

The second area in which Lotus went against the trend was in not adopting gas-filled dampers. They worked conscientiously with Armstrong, using conventional hydraulic units, yet achieved the usual legendary Lotus combination of ride and unmatched handling.

Whilst the reasoning behind the non-adoption of trendy gas dampers was just that they did not need them, the thought behind the solid discs was rather more convoluted. Basically it seemed to come down to a lack of faith in manufacturing standards and a nagging worry that there would be another source of vibration and kick-back to fight. This was a struggle they need not undertake

Sturdy and comfortable steering wheel sits in front of the Turbo dashboard layout, which is distinguished by the central boost gauge

85

The 20,000th Lotus 16-valve road engine was this turbocharged example. Left to right are the engine team who have been involved throughout the production run: Barrie Greengrass, Frank Harris and Bernard Bland. The engine was produced in 1981, a decade after the original 140 bhp units went out to Jensen

since their comparatively light car (2690 lb claimed) performed in exemplary fashion with its four wheel solid disc system.

Finally on the chassis side there was one worrying specification change. The initial car I drove, and the first Essex cars, came on three piece Compomotive alloy wheels. Unfortunately there were problems with them, and the car's specification was amended to take BBS Mahle alloy wheels, which having a 15 in. diameter, raised the gearing to nearly 23 mph per 1000 rpm: the fronts are 7J and the rears 8J.

Although some prototype testing was conducted on Pirelli low profile tyres, Goodyear NCTs always looked like being the final choice, as Lotus had such close links with the American-owned giant. Goodyear had put in a very fine effort to ensure that their rather stiff cover associated well with the light Lotus. With the benefit of hindsight I would say Goodyear provided an excellent cover for Lotus, especially in the wet where the legendary handling abilities can still be explored with confidence, something that can be said of no other 150 mph plus mid-engine car of my acquaintance, save the BMW M1.

Tyre sizes echoed the original S1 with a 195 preferred at the front, but of 60 per cent aspect ratio, while the rears were also VR-rated at 235/60.

The interior was also reworked by Giugiaro. The biggest impact came from the standard ruche-stitched leather seats (optional on non-Essex models), but also much commented on was the four speaker Panasonic roof-mounted FM radio and cassette player. Air conditioning became standard on Essex, optional later, and the controls were shifted to a centre console panel, with backlit switchgear when the exterior lights were in use.

The instrument panel was slightly re-arranged to accommodate a central boost gauge (reading in lb as well as atmospheres) and a 170 mph speedometer. Instrument lighting went back to those restful green shades of the S1, while the still large steering wheel was a touch more elegant than the S1's and S2's, having a thinner two-spoke layout and leather rim of confidence-building 'bunginess'.

Performance

The press were just allowed road impressions of the original Essex Turbo, but a test car (OPW 667W) of the less expensive non-Essex versions trickled through to many users and had done 27,000 miles by late 1981. That car proved capable of reaching 60 mph from rest in 6.1s and 100 mph in 17s when driven by *Autocar* tester and former Lotus works driver John Miles. Top speed was measured at 149 mph at 6600 rpm in fifth, with an overall consumption of 18 mpg after a very hard test, which included Continental mileage.

That test was simply headed 'Paragon of the Turbocharged' but *Motor* went even further, nicknaming the test car 'White Heat', a tag that stuck inside the factory.

Factory figures were 210 bhp at 6000 rpm, with 200 lb ft. torque. This gave 0–60 mph in 5.55s; 0–100 mph in 14.65s and a maximum of 152 mph. The quarter mile times were very close, *Autocar* reporting 14.6s at 94 mph terminal speed and Lotus 14.4s and 98 mph.

With April 1981's announcement of the non-Essex Turbo at prices from under £17,000, Lotus also claimed mpg figures from 19.7 urban to 38.7 mpg at a constant 56 mph. *Autocar* were a lot more modest and reckoned 15.7 mpg as the urban figure and 28.4 mpg as the constant 56 mph figure. My own experiences are related in the final chapter, but one should not forget that Lotus were offering a 150 mph supercar with 20 mpg capabilities, something that deserved a niche in automotive history at the time, never mind the incredible handling and braking capabilities.

Overall, the Turbo Esprit is too recent a development to permit comment at great length on its service life. We do know that the galvanised chassis, with five year anti-corrosion warranty amongst its previously mentioned attractions, was a distinct step forward upon the Lotus road to international recognition.

The engine was not totally satisfactory in its original development guise, being badly served by a variety of wastegates that would close in the self-destruct position. The problem here was that there had been no room in the original design to fit a separate wastegate in amongst the rear suspension and entwining exhaust. At one stage Lotus were even getting wastegates supplied from Australia, but the situation in early 1982 was that they were available from Garrett themselves in Los

Angeles. This looked as though it had helped the situation greatly. In service only three Turbo wastegate-related problems had been reported by April 1982.

There were some carburettor problems too during development sealing the throttle spindles and float chambers. The fuel pump, intended to give a constant supply at $4\frac{1}{2}$ lb above boost pressure was sometimes let down by the pressure regulator valve too.

Lotus are not the kind of people to let details get them down—nor are the customers, to judge by the positively booming production of the Turbo model in early 1982. By the close of 1981 some 173 had been made since the official inception of production in March 1980.

For the future of the installation Lotus were full of plans. A higher compression looked likely and, if the £120,000 could be found for the silicon chip technology to control an engine electronics management system, then that looked a likely fitment on future Turbos, too.

In leaving the Turbo one may ponder the fate of the V8 motor. The Esprit had been running way back in the seventies with an eight cylinder engine in the back, but it was the Rover V8 that was initially assessed and the upset to the handling of a sensitive Lotus was considerable (remember also the GKN Rover V8 Europa?). This weakness, plus an increasing awareness of the price and scarcity of oil, kept the eight at bay. I can tell you, unofficially, that it is an approximate doubling up of the original 2-litre to 4 litres. Prototypes have been running for some years with a flexible 320 bhp and good mpg results, but production seemed some development time away at the time of writing.

Returning to 1980 we shall see it was a busy year for normally aspirated Esprits too. . . .

Chapter 7
Series 2.2:
the rarest Esprit

Just two months were to elapse before another Esprit derivative was put into production—in April 1980. Formally announced in May of that year, the Esprit Series 2.2 became the model with the shortest run so far (even less than some specific 'limited edition' models!) for production ceased in March 1981, after only 86* Series 2.2s had been made.

As a model it caused a certain amount of wincing when mentioned at Hethel, but large Lotus retail dealers Bell and Colvill in Surrey were kinder about the model, and allowed me to browse around their stock to highlight some of the Esprit changes over the years. Co-founder and historic racing buff R. H. 'Bobby' Bell helped fill in some of the gaps on the S2.2, and his comments have been taken into account. Since Bell and Colvill also marketed their own Turbo Esprit some years before Lotus, I listened with special attention.

The S2.2 was not a failure in the way that its short run might suggest, but a logical stop gap introduced until the improved chassis and rear suspension of the Turbo could be offered, together with some other detail improvements that genu-

Lotus' later records show 46 constucted! See Appendices.

91

inely did cut costs in its successor, the 1981 S3.

In simple terms, the 2.2 was simply the longer-stroke 2172 cc engine allied to the original S1 and S2 chassis with driveshafts acting as a top link in the rear suspension. The body, including the wrap around spoiler in matt black and the air ducting 'ears' for the engine bay, was identical to the S2's. So was the engine hatch with rear section holding wheelbrace and jack, and hinge upwards to give partial access to the engine in order to check oil and water levels without total removal. Neat, but not the final answer to the inevitable problems associated with mid engines.

Underneath the body there was an important long term change, in that the galvanised chassis with a five year warranty was introduced. This often leads to confusion as the Turbo chassis was also offered with this warranty and treatment. So it is wise to reiterate that the 2.2 shared the earlier chassis design.

For Lotus engineers it was not a simple case of 'popping-in the 2.2 and changing the badges'. As Colin Spooner told me, 'we went up on clutch specification and that demanded casing alterations. Then the exhaust system had to be changed if we were going to get the best out of the bigger engine, so that demanded another system with appropriate bore sizes and free flow characteristics to get over any increased back pressure.

'Then there was the engine itself. There were real NVH roughness problems with the extra stroke motor and we tried to get over these with new mountings.' Mike Kimberley was especially knowledgeable in the field of rubber bushings for suspension and engine mountings, because of his Jaguar experience. There they also used a driveshaft top link rear suspension but in a totally different application.

Colin Spooner continued, 'there were a series of

longitudinal vibrations from the crankshaft of the 2.2 and this gave us quite severe driveline problems to overcome. The flexible flywheel approach with the ring gear outside helped, but we also had to face a number of airborne resonances in the cockpit and tackle these with a change in the sound deadening materials.' Spooner recalled.

From the 1971 Jensen production through the 1978 2.2 litre stretch for Talbot to the introduction of the bigger unit for their own purposes Lotus reckoned to have made 18,000 of their 16-valve engines by the spring of 1980: in December 1981 they celebrated production of the 20,000th unit.

For the Esprit (and simultaneously for the Eclat/Elite) the Type 912 motor was subtly changed from that supplied to Talbot. The prin-

The Bell & Colvill turbocharged Esprit was widely tested by the motoring press prior to the arrival of the factory model. The conversion cost £2000 in 1978, bringing a total car cost to £11,700 and was totally different to the 1980 factory car, including a single large SU carburettor upstream of the turbocharger. Quoted power output was 210 bhp, the same as the factory figure, with 202 lb ft of torque. The conversion work was by Stuart Mathieson of former Mathwall and Alan Mann Racing repute

Esprit S2.2 continued the Series 2 look but the enlarged engine offered both an extra measure of power and fuel economy

ciples: bore and stroke, 9.4:1 cr, twin Dell'Orto 45 DHLA carburettors and all alloy construction remained common. For the USA twin CD 175SE carburettors and an 8.4:1 cr were key factors in a strangled unit that made 140 bhp at 5800 rpm and 130 lb ft. torque, all on 91 octane lead-free fuel.

On paper there was exactly 10 bhp difference between Talbot and Lotus 2.2: some 160 bhp at 6500 rpm and 160 lb ft. torque at 5000 revs for Lotus. For Talbot? The quote was 150 bhp at 5600 rpm and 147 lb ft. torque at 4800 rpm. It is worth pointing out that the 2.2 litre Lotus engine is said to give the same 140 lb ft. of torque that was originally credited to the 2-litre, but the 2.2 manages this at 2400 rpm instead of 4900 revs!

Much of the improvement over the original 2-litre and the Talbot application can be credited to the type 107 camshaft that has been employed on the Lotus in-house version of the 2.2 engine, this offering fractionally more lift; plus timing that complements more recent Lotus thinking on combustion in an emission age, as well as working with electronic ignition in the Lotus application.

Other fundamental differences between Lotus and Talbot applications are primarily at the bottom end. The Talbot required a front well sump, the Lotus wet sump arrangement being with the well at the rear of the motor—mounting being completely different, of course, as well as the intrusion of a crossmember in the Talbot application. Both Talbot and Lotus 2.2s have strengthened main bearing panels, but they are not interchangeable main bearing castings.

The Speedline manufactured Lotus wheel, the standard fitment for S2 and 2.2 in 7 JK × 14 front guise. The rears were 7½ JK × 14

2.2 action

The big improvement offered by 2.2 was flexibility, but Bobby Bell tells me that there was a fuel economy bonus in routine traffic driving too. Lotus claimed some 20 per cent better mpg and supplied these figures (the 2-litre Esprit S2 is in brackets): City, 19.7 mpg (18.6); constant 56 mph, 38.7 mpg (37.7) and constant 75 mph, 33.3 mpg (31.3).

Similarly Lotus figures for performance were as overleaf. They represent the standard 4:1 final drive, in mph and seconds.

The decalling department at Lotus is rarely idle!

Top right *A rear beast at rest. Less than 100 of S2.2 were made and they can be regarded as a good potential investment, besides having many practical and desirable improvements over earlier models*

Acceleration	Esprit 2.2	Esprit S2
0–30	2.4	2.6
0–40	3.5	3.7
0–50	5.0	5.6
0–60	6.7	7.3
0–70	8.9	10.1
0–80	11.3	12.8
0–90	14.8	16.3
0–100	19.2	21.5
Fifth gear		
30–50	13.0	14.4
40–60	7.5	13.6
50–70	8.4	12.9
60–80	9.3	13.8
70–90	8.3	15.7
80–100	8.6	16.6

I have quoted these at length because they are more realistic than earlier Lotus claims. Maxima were given as 40, 60, 88 and 120 mph at 7000 rpm in the first four gears with 138 mph given as the maximum still. Now the Esprit could genuinely get over 130 in fifth.

From a collector's viewpoint the badging was simply altered to read Esprit 2.2 and there were no longer number designations for option packages, a Lotus practice that had spread from Elite to S2 Esprit.

The 2.2 litre installation underlined the fact that a number of problems could be tackled by switching to the Turbo type chassis and rear suspension. Yet it was not only the engineering appeal of changing Esprit's simple suspension to take updated Lotus chassis backbone technology, there was also cost to consider.

Consider: the Esprit 2.2 was introduced at £14,951 in late May 1980. When it went out of production it cost £15,270. A look at the March 1981 issue of *Autocar* detailing that Esprit 2.2

Bottom right *Series 2 and 2.2 wrap-round front spoiler with the normal Dunlop 205/60 VR 14 radials mounted on Speedline-Lotus wheels*

price also shows that a Porsche 924 Turbo (tested to 140 mph and acclaimed as very economical at 19.8 mpg overall) was 'only' £13,998. Even a legend like the 911 SC, increasingly well equipped as the Pound strengthened against the Dm (instead of price cutting and reducing prestige) retailed for less than two thousand pounds more than the Lotus at £16,732.

For added perspective the £15,000 plus Esprit fitted into a market where Ferrari's 308 paralleled the £20,000 level of the Esprit Essex Turbo, while the 2.8 litre TVR Tasmin was yours for under

Three spoke sports wheel is a nice feature of this LHD drive special edition Esprit

£13,000 and the Jaguar XJ-S at an official £19,763. This and other Jaguar models were so widely discounted that you could easily buy one for less than the Lotus. It was a market situation Lotus had to act upon, especially as the worldwide situation was far worse. In the attractive markets like the USA, Porsche came in with competitive models at almost half a Lotus's list price.

Although Lotus were doing Very Nicely Thank You on the engineering side, they could now also make more cars. So far as the Esprit and its elegant front-engined sisters were concerned the priority was clear. Complete the impossible. Produce a better car for less money!

Chapter 8
Cheaper means better

A week after a Turbo was announced for less than £17,000, Lotus struck another blow at the bemused British market—a market which could have been described in April 1981 as one in a state of catatonic shock so far as luxury or high performance vehicles outside the West German establishment were concerned. Lotus were in much the same state of recession themselves. Engineering continued to do well with a variety of clients to replace De Lorean and Talbot, though I understand the De Lorean deal was a one off of such financial worth that it will never be repeated. Yet the manufacturing side had suffered the cruellest of setbacks and was still game for an aggressive comeback.

The 'cruellest of setbacks?' What would you call the total loss of the biggest export market, and the biggest market for the Esprit? So far as making and selling new cars was concerned, Lotus had no purchases from their trading partners Rolls-Royce during the 1981 season! I am *not* implying any fault on the Rolls side, just stating a fact.

Apparently the Lotus dealer organisation in the USA was in such a terrible state that the

Colour conscious S3 displays the way in which the spoiler and lower sills were spray matched to the body colour. Example shown here has the popular option of turbo-style BBS Mahle wheels and Goodyear NCT tyres

company simply could not go on selling through their existing network: thus the September 1979 marketing deal with Rolls for the USA. I don't know the ins and outs of what happened in America, just that no Lotuses were required by Rolls from Lotus in 1981; a package of over 300 units for the States was being negotiated when this book went to press, so the association was not over. Quite the contrary, it sounds as though it had just taken much longer than Lotus had imagined to set the American house in order before sales could recommence, Rolls-Royce or no Rolls-Royce.

The pressure had been on for Lotus to do something about the UK, now that their overseas outlets were so effectively corked. They started looking really hard at reducing costs. There were redundancies and all the other horrors of the recession, but the benefit was a tough look at that

popular word 'rationalisation', and what it could mean to Lotus.

For the Esprit it meant a much better product at a lower price, for the decision was taken to incorporate Turbo chassis and rear suspension technology in a new S3, normally aspirated, 2.2 Esprit.

For £13,461 the normal Esprit customer finally got all the benefits of that top link rear suspension and the feeling of total integrity provided by the new chassis, for it also carried that Elite/Eclat descended Lotus wishbone and lower link front springing. Spring rates were softened (by 10 per cent) from the original but the Armstrong dampers remained in situ. The main reason for re-rating was the drop in weight from Turbo's 2690 lb to the S3's official 2244 lb. Incidentally, the plunging drive shaft rear suspension with its optional BBS Mahle Turbo wheels carrying the

Rear end revision included the word LOTUS embossed into the back bumper and yet another task for Lotus decal department with 'Esprit 3' badge and another stripe derivative. Underneath was a very much better and cheaper motor car

Turbo's Goodyear NCTs, stretches the rear track by 0.7 in. and the front by an inch exactly. You could still get the Speedline alloys as standard equipment (now shod with 205/60 VR 14 front Goodyear NCTs and 205/70 VR 14 rears instead of Dunlop), but the optional 15-in. BBS wheels with widths of 7 in. at the front and an inch wider at the rear were very popular on the stock we saw in 1982.

In fact the S3 and Turbo were by then much more popular than preceding Esprits had ever been, the price cut for a better product catching a lot of attention and leading to such an increase in credibility that many of the cars leaving the 27 main Lotus UK dealerships in 1982 were back up to the old basic price levels, but this time they were fully equipped and much better detailed cars.

Examples—walk round a current S3 and you immediately note a high standard of metallic paint finish, and the fit of doors and boot hatch is nicer, though it is still internally released on the SR by T-bar and cable. On Turbos there is a separate external lock, which has a revised air dam section. Open the tail hatch and you are struck by the neat zip-cover storage aft of a well fitted engine cover that can either be swung up or lifted out to allow exceptionally good access to the engine.

Visually the S3 looks a more integrated car than previous series largely because the boy racer use of matt black paint is gone and the spoiler and restyled lower sill panels are now sprayed in body colour. The 'ears' behind the rear side windows are incorporated into the car in a similar way, but are also better blended in. They still feed air directly to the carburettors, but the general engine air feed comes into the bay aft of the carburettors on S3 and in front on S2.

Bumpers curving around the corners of the car

and carrying the large LOTUS legend embossed into the rear are part of S3s visual identification. Lockable fuel filler caps became standard on this model.

Aerodynamically, there are only the fractional differences that we have come to expect on this model: compared to Turbo's 0.342, an 0.34 factor was reported by management. To report this on its own is to miss the point that Lotus expertise in under car engineering is not so absent as one

S3 interior picked up everything from the Turbo except the boost gauge which identifies this car

103

might think from these bland details. They prefer not to discuss what they do. Anyone with eyes and motorsport experience should be able to fathom that what Lotus do with air under a road car is far from leaving it to mill about uselessly! Developments on this side were unfortunately scheduled for a big publicity boost after this book went to press, so suffice it to say that Esprit was and is one of the first cars to take notice of what was happening underneath as well as above. This is, after all, only the way it should be, considering Lotus's pioneering work with ground-effect machinery in motor racing.

Air management inside the S3 engine bay also utilised convection effects to draw in outside air, even when the car was stationary.

The engine itself remained unchanged, save for flexible exhaust piping joints and a degree of extra silencing. Perhaps the most important aspect here was that Lotus could mount the engine to take account of NVH, as the top link of the rear suspension took any requirement for side loading rigidity away. Lotus took full advantage of this and the result was a much smoother performance altogether.

The braking specification was still shared with Turbo, which meant that compared to an S1, the S3 offered 10.5 in. diameter front discs instead of the 9.7 in. units that were used from the S1 to the S2.2. At the rear, the 10.8 in. S2 diameter remained, also shared with Turbo. The vented disc units are still relegated to the experimental shelves.

Inside an S3

The interior of the Esprit always was an exciting cockpit but the S3, whether trimmed in the now much smarter velour fabrics, or the optional combinations of half or full leather trim, approaches a stylist's triumph. The steering wheel is now the inch smaller and neater Turbo two-spoke affair, as is the 170 mph speedometer also derived from the Turbo/S3 rationalisation. The seat-backs and steering are still strictly non-adustable, but in practice seem to offer a wide range of customers extraordinary satisfaction. Visibility is still limited, but this is an inherent part of such lines.

Aside from allowing the engine mountings to fulfil more of an insulation role, Lotus also provided a considerable dose of extra sound-proofing, claimed to produce a 50 per cent reduction of interior noise levels. It seems fair to comment that, whereas boom and resonance was always a problem right up to the S2 form, the S2.2 showed a determined attempt to tackle the problem. The S3 got it as right as one could reasonably expect of a large four cylinder sports motor nestling behind the occupants' ears.

Other standard cabin equipment in the S3 included speakers built into the doors and variable instrument lighting—the latter was applied by slide switch gear. The price in June 1981 was £13,513 for each of the 152 completed examples but had risen to £13,700 by January 1982.

Incidentally, the reason that so many S3s were sold, with the optional 15-in. wheel equipment from BBS Mahle, was the moderate extra cost of under £90. In some other cars of this price range, such wheels and tyres could amount to a £1000 option.

Bottom end of current 2.2 motor has considerable strengthening precautions added to original design. Many of the engine manufacturing processes at Lotus are computer controlled, matching the technical sophistication of design

Driving impressions

A crowded forecourt, jammed with Saabs and Alfa Romeos, as well as a barely de-waxed, 43-mile-old,

Esprit S3; that was the sight which greeted me at Bell & Colvill, West Horsley one hazy February day. Barely a month after my visit to try and unravel some mysteries of S2.2 proprietors Bobby Bell and Martin Colvill had decided to fill the gap in my Esprit experience. Lotus had by then sold their press demonstrator!

The metallic blue example was very new indeed, so I avoided prolonged high rpm. That led me straight into an outstanding facet of the 2.2 carburettor engine's abilities. As you would expect torque and general civilisation are sharply improved over the early 2-litre. This twin carburettor unit, lacking even a pre-delivery check, was one of the best examples of sweet pulling power in a performance engine, injected or carburated, that it has been my pleasure to try. Not once did it stall from its cold start. Then, once running at its normal 90°C it provided enough sparkle between 3000 and 4000 rpm to see the wide blue Lotus scuttling through bumpy B-roads at astounding and unprintable speeds. Occasionally over 4500 rpm was needed to exit a slow corner neatly, but generally the engine displayed rock confident 74 lb oil pressure and that rarest of alliances in big fours: impressive torque and eagerness to stretch for high revs.

Cabin noise was down, but there was rather more of it from around the door seals than remembered, probably because of the interior noise level reductions! A great improvement inside is the use of the smaller Turbo steering wheel, but the visibility and laid-back driving position do require more than a 30 mile test burst to acquire a natural 'Esprit de corps'.

Just as Lotus executives had promised, I came back feeling that S3 is probably a better bet for 90 per cent of customers than the Esprit Turbo. Response is immediate from the engine and the

Lotus Esprit Series 3

The Esprit Series 3 answers the challenging standards set by Grand Prix racing with the kind of performance and style you expect from the exclusive Lotus pedigree of 7 World Champion Car Constructor titles.

Now the only true British sports car in the grand tradition – a practical mid-engined 2-seater – it combines the exhilaration of a 138 mph top speed with outstandingly distinctive exterior styling and exclusive standards of interior luxury.

You'll admire the Esprit Series 3 response to your driving demands: the excitement of 0-60 acceleration in 6.7 seconds, the perfection of its steering and braking precision, matched by the internationally acclaimed safety features of the body and chassis design that helped Lotus models win the DON Safety Trophy. Only the comfort of your ride reminds you that the Esprit Series 3 has been exclusively designed to give you the spirit of the race track – on the road.

The Esprit Series 3 is a direct result of the effects of Lotus' continuous engineering programme; which introduces new specifications throughout the production run of a model. Visual style and engineering improvements produce greater aerodynamic efficiency, economy and performance –

the drag co-efficient of 0.33 is in part a result of continuous wind-tunnel testing.

Long-term assessment and running chassis evaluation have led to a thrilling and comfortable ride – with the sound insulation barrier reducing cockpit noise levels dramatically.

chassis seems even better balanced at low speeds (below 85 mph) than that of the Turbo, coming from the beefy 2.2 pulling response in the 2500–5000 rpm band. As an experiment we drove away smoothly from 1400 rpm in fourth, finding that the feeling is of more response than in the Turbo subjected to the same test.

In short it takes an S3 Esprit to highlight what was wrong with the original and place Lotus as firmly in advance of their rivals in the ride and handling stakes as they were with S1.

Of course there are snags, hopefully all mentioned in this book. Yet for the self made, comparatively young man, there can be few more

The S3 brochure quotes an 0.33 aerodynamic drag factor, 138 mph maximum and 0–60 mph in 6.7. The performance claims were very closely matched by Autocar's road test results in 1981

The Esprit 3 we tried had the optional larger wheels and tyres, providing a convincing demonstration of why many insiders feel this is simply the best Lotus yet, Turbo included

exhilarating experiences than achieving Esprit ownership. A car for use in the intended role of pleasure-provider rather than daily business barge.

Esprit in the Eighties

'Aggressive pricing? I suppose you could say that, but I would prefer to say that wc had to get to the point where our products, Esprit included, were generally perceived as superb value for money against their opposition. Not particularly one brand like Porsche. To be honest I don't think we hurt them much [Porsche sell over 2000 vehicles a year in the UK] but I think we were knocking Ferrari quite hard. We picked up three of their dealers in recent months and now our production is sold out until the end of March.' That was Roger Putnam, sales director of Lotus Cars, talking in January 1982.

By then the Esprit S3 was up to £13,781.90 basic and Putnam could look forward to selling around 600 Esprits in 1982. About half would go to the UK, but 20 would end up in RHD form in Japan. If all went well another 20 would follow, making Lotus Britain's second biggest car exporter to that country!

The Esprit was also to be sold in all the Common Market countries, and through much of the rest of Europe, including places like Portugal and Austria. Canadian exports were a fact, while America looked like coming on stream again (but with a Dell'Orto equipped 2.2) from July 1982 with 20 units a month produced, half of them Turbos. The latter had been privately imported like exotic Ferraris through a back door in California, but that loophole had been closed by January 1982. The Far and Middle East were also Esprit customers, while negotiations were going on to get back into Australia when this was written.

When I called Esprit production was split into 20–23 of the S3 every month, 16 of those earmarked for UK, and the rest for export. Turbo Esprits were running a slightly higher volume of a consistent 24 per month, with roughly the same home and export market split, but volume was set to increase sharply from the 385 employees who had weathered the worst of the recession with Lotus.

Chapter 9
Series 007:
the Bond Esprits

'I reckon it cost us about the price of a one page colour ad in the *Sunday Times*, roughly £14,000.' That was Donovan McLauchlan, Lotus PR, recollecting the costs of attaining that dream for any motor manufacturer: exposure in a major TV series or film. That remark specifically covers the use of two Lotus Esprit Turbos and one £4000 two-month construction of a mock Turbo to blow into eternity for the James Bond film *For Your Eyes Only*. Lotus were also involved in the 1977 Bond movie *The Spy Who Loved Me*. On this occasion probably up to £18,000 was expended on two roadgoing S1s and five bodyshells, one of which eventually made a 7 knot submarine! How did it all come about?

McLauchlan takes up the story of how Lotus tried to break into the film world, although it was not easy to follow the Aston Martins, BSA 650 motorcycles and Ford Mustangs of earlier Bond movies, that was the original objective. Don explains, 'In the seventies I spent some time down at Pinewood knocking on doors trying to get into a major TV series. My offer of loaning my company Lotus for a week or so didn't really compare with offers like the fleet of BL cars that were used on series like the *New Avengers*!

'A contact tipped me the nod that a Bond movie was scheduled for Pinewood production shortly. So, during 1975, I took down a pre-production Esprit to the Studios, dropped a quid to the doorman and left the Esprit prototype right in the path of anyone trying to get in or out! During the day I parked it in various visible spots and then just drove off into the sunset. Naturally people asked what the car was, and eventually it got to the right ears and I got a phone call. By late 1975 I had met with Cubby Broccoli and we were in business!'

The unmodified S1 Esprits, two of them, went to work in Sardinia for high jinks that included squirting 'cement' over pursuing baddies. In fact just four nozzles were fitted beneath a movable number plate to imply that, in fact they were dumping the loads of grey porridge oats that actually came from a separate truck and hose. Lotus drivers in this Bond spectacular included 'Don Mac' and Roger Becker, the test driving chief, covering much of the high speed mileage.

Perhaps the star was the Perry submarine, Bahamas, conversion of Esprit shell into submarine. Lotus did quite a lot of basic work, including installing fins and the like. They used to get their part-marinized shells back regularly with cryptic notes like: 'Brace engine bay for

The Lotus badge department were not about to pass by an opportunity like the James Bond film appearances. PPW 306R was part of the cast of The Spy Who Loved Me *and is still retained by Lotus for show work*

Above *Corfu, filming* For Your Eyes Only *with the original white Turbo Esprit*

Above right *Ready for blast off!* For Your Eyes Only *film crew prepare the dummy Esprit for exploding oblivion. Note the touch up paint and big hammers, vital equipment for hasty transformations, plus the straggling wires and cork board for extra destructive effects*

rocket thrust', and 'Adjust periscope aperture'. When such job lists were read off during public tours of the works, it caused endless amusement.

However the 'submarinisation' was down to Perrys and a $100,000 budget just for this aspect of the film turned the Esprit shell into a 7 knot, four electric motor sub, complete with ballast tanks and joystick controls. One severe handicap of the Lotus shape was that it was designed for down-force, which meant it was a job to keep off the ocean floor!

Another of the five shells was equipped with a simple compressed air rocket, and was fired off a pier at 45 mph, complete with simple spaceframe and locked steering. . . .

Something like a year of Lotus effort went into the first Bond movie, the cars only modified (the road cars, that is!) with an extra skin beneath the front radiator to protect them over rougher Sardinian going. One car was simply sold anonymously: the other (PPW 306R) is with the company to this day, and is still in rude health after a life of public appearances and film work.

Part II

The Turbo Esprit was a natural for a Bond movie. Again Lotus used two road cars, but this time they came in white with brown leather upholstery for the Corfu-filmed section of *For Your Eyes Only* and then returned to Hethel to become metallic copper, born again with cream Connolly leather upholstery for the filming in the ski resort of Cortina.

Why? The original white car (OPW 654W) had to be blown up! After two months' hard labour, a mock-up with doors and glass attached so that they would blow out in one piece was the result. Such a job is a lot more complex than you might think, for the car has to look real yet use the minimum number of parts to lower destruction costs. All that was left from the shell itself was a singed 3 in. by 8 in. frazzle....

When the two white cars came back for their transformation to brown, they obviously had to have a different number as Bond's replacement to the exploding white Turbo. Thus two brown Turbos, driven for much of the footage by Lotus men McLauchlan and chief test driver Roger Becker, went to Cortina bearing the plates OPW 654W (not for filming of course) and OPW 678W, a registration then just for filming. Today OPW 654W is on McLauchlan's company car, with a red warning triangle to remind one of the number plate's explosive past, while the other car from the Bond epic was simply sold. The second registration lives on, presently attached to a blue engineering S3.

Roger Moore and Esprit at the Cortina ski resort. Non standard items included the rear ski racks and white highlights for rear bumper and Goodyear tyres. The car was one of the resprayed original white machines from Corfu

The Turbos in *For Your Eyes Only* were largely unmodified save for attachments to hold Bond's skis and cut outs for the brake lights (Bond must never brake: he's too brave!) and the radio aerials, which would otherwise cause continuity problems by bobbing up and down out of sequence!

Lotus are obviously well pleased with the results of their association with the Bond movies, but from personal commercial and filming experience I would advise budding publicists that the amount of detail and time involved in getting any action sequence shot, even just a few seconds in length, is an unbelievable drain on man hours, patience and company demonstrators. The film and TV game is only for those who understand and accept such facts of an apparently glamorous life.

Chapter 10
How was it in there?

Esprits mean most to me as the only mid-engine cars outside Fiat's X1/9 and BMW's M1 that I have enjoyed driving on public roads with a feeling of total safety. Not only safe, they also put a grin on your face, whatever model! Other allegedly more prestigious names have left behind memories of sudden clammy hands and the premonition that *this* time I was not going to get away with a change of conditions in mid corner, or a straightforward excess of speed into a curve. On the track a mid-engine layout is traditional and supremely safe, and perhaps this is why Lotus are so good at the roadgoing translation of the theory.

The Esprit does not have a factory competition history, but has been campaigned with varying degrees of honour and calamity by privateers. Perhaps the nearest the Esprit came to motorsport was years before its inception when the Lotus 62 was being campaigned, with the iron block version of the 16-valve engine using Tecalemit-Jackson fuel injection. 'It might well have had the claimed 220 bhp,' recorded former works driver John Miles, 'but it was so wide and had such a frontal area it was hard pushed to keep up with 180 bhp Chevrons. Still the engine was very reliable, ran like a train it did.' Which was more than could be said for the all-alloy Lotus Formula 2 version of the engine in the back of those Texaco Stars. 'Nuff said, back to our Esprits. . . .

My first driving encounter with an Esprit came in the closing months of 1976. A white example was provided for a quick dash round the Hethel track in company with Denis Jenkinson. I was overawed in this company (you keep thinking he must be thinking 'my God, Stirling would be changing up here, not panic braking!') but it was apparent that the basic handling was far in advance of the opposition. It was also immediately obvious that the four cylinder noise and resonance problem was so serious as to border on the unacceptable and that there was a fair degree of understeer through steering of less feel than was the Lotus tradition.

Looking back today, the driving characteristics that have struck the driver so forcibly over the years have been fixed back seating and steering offering exceptional comfort and precision; the thickness of the front screen pillars; the odd and largely ineffective handbrake to the right in the righthand door sill of the RHD Esprits, and the normal rear and threequarter rear vision problems which are made worse on the Turbo models by the rear window slats.

In the original S1 the feeling of being 'laid back' was the strongest because such a formula car racing stance had not been widely offered frequently on road cars before. Although the Esprit S1 was exciting, I found this laid back seating led to a sense of detachment that sharply improved my rather volatile driving style. You could sense when a traffic opportunity was genuine rather than jinking around like the pilot of a hot saloon, upsetting everyone.

The 907 engine in alleged 160 bhp form (I say that because 155 bhp had been quoted around the same period too) proved better silenced than I had expected by the time of my first full road test, published in *Motoring News*, August 25, 1977. With the benefit of hindsight I would say I was over-enthusiastic about the car at that stage: the original test session had produced a fuel pump failure after five laps, and I suffered the frequent indignity of push starts in the '77 S1 too, one of them with the aid of Jaguar staff at Browns Lane!

It was actually a combination of brakes, handling and a reasonably powerful engine in a light, wide (oh boy was it *wide*!) car that led to unbeatable A to B averages. Searing power was not the impression, but 90 mph at an indicated 4000 rpm was a pace that the Esprit chassis shrugged off on B-roads, unsorted rear suspension notwithstanding! About 120 mph was the fastest the car seemed happiest at (shown as 5500 revs) in fifth, so it will not come as any surprise to hear that I lost my licence in it, trying to peer over a friend's briefcase obscuring that interesting Armada of West London police we had in tow! It was a bright yellow, and I still loved it, especially as I managed to get 26 mpg overall out of it via so many long-legged cruising trips outside London.

Buying: new-Turbo Esprit

Gathered from my impressions at the time and from subsequent conversations with the trade, I would be inclined to leave the S1 and the S2 well alone today, unless the car is bought purely as a fun vehicle by a knowledgeable owner-mechanic. That rear suspension design led to wheel bearing and driveshaft problems, and some of the 50,000 mile S1s I have seen have suffered badly with corroded wheels, and rusty window surrounds. As ever, any light coloured upholstery tends to look

Longtime Lotus supporter, former Elan exponent Richard Jenvey ensured that the Esprit appeared in World Championship endurance racing in 1979

really dog-eared after four or five years' use, even at only 10,000 miles a year.

The S2.2 is a different matter. Not because it is a better design; in many ways the combination of 2.2 litres and the old chassis is to be deplored, but because it is simply younger. Bobby Bell was particularly persuasive in the model's defence, and the 10,000 mile example I looked at (some £11,500 when I investigated, early in 1982) was as like a new car as it should have been, *except* in the engine bay. Here there were the usual leaks and poor detailing; always a Lotus weakness, which can be particularly depressing when it's your money buying such a glamorous exterior.

Still the S2.2 has yet another strong card to

play: rarity. At less than 100 cars produced, and with a good trade reputation for much improved reliability, plus the rather overlooked role it has played owing to the subsequent swift introduction of the S3, could turn the 2.2s into hot property as the years go by. Certainly that 2.2 engine is everything that Lotus claimed at the time, providing truly flexible performance, leading to urban fuel consumption gains and superb overtaking abilities out of town.

S3? Yes, much, *much* better. If you can afford it, the S3 is a genuine improvement that Lotus are firmly convinced will turn into the classic Esprit. Chassis behaviour with the optional Turbo 15-in. wheels and tyres is reportedly even better than Turbo's owing to the slight weight reduction and instant response of the latest 2.2 engine. All this and 21.7 mpg overall even including the performance testing period at *Autocar.*

Turbo: blows the mind, as well as the carbs

I have driven both the Essex, the original £21,000 commemorative job and a very slightly less elaborate Turbo Esprit, the latter for a week (*MN*, July 2, 1981).

Again there's that special feeling of conducting an aircraft on the ground, this time enhanced by the twitching boost gauge and acceleration that really does credit to Esprit's superb chassis and brakes. If you can drive it properly, remembering to feed power in gradually rather than just planting your foot squarely on the floor abruptly, it is an economical device, as well as a genuine supercar. I got just above and just below 20 mpg driving hard, whenever the considerable police attention waned. In fact the car is such an eye-catcher that you have to drive it sensibly, or pay the consequences of owning something that looks like it is breaking the sound barrier, even when crawling through city streets.

Perhaps the triumph of the Turbo is how Lotus have got a comparatively simple turbocharger and chassis layout to perform better than anything which had been seen up to its introduction. Senior Development Test Driver, Roger Becker, did a considerable mileage at speeds of over 130 mph, so if you do get the opportunity to drive it really hard there shouldn't be any problems, however hot the pace, or the climate.

My outstanding memories of the Turbo are of the integrated, honest, feel the new chassis gave the whole car, plus its stunning wet weather performance. Whistling up, down, round, over and even under the crags of the Yorkshire moors in a thunderstorm was sheer delight. Occasionally the back Goodyears would slither out of line on standing water under full throttle. Then the steering had literally only to be eased, rather than tweaked into a full opposite lock attitude, in order to put everything neatly and rapidly back 'in order'.

I loved the car and I should think Lotus still love it for what the Turbo Esprit did for their reputation.

Buying Turbo

With only just over 170 vehicles made and an introduction date in 1980 you might not feel there was much to say. Wrong, but I have to compress it.

Watch out for the type of wheels fitted and the fact that the original Essex model was over £20,000. When buying secondhand, I would advise steering clear of the Essex series, unless you particularly want their colours, or fancy that the limited run makes it a collectors' item.

There were some problems with wastegate suppliers in development, the first batch showing a tendency toward jamming in the shut position and thus damaging the engine severely if the sharply escalating boost gauge was not promptly observed. A second type from Australia was not wholly satisfactory either, but the 1982 model year production with Garrett wastegate equipment is considered satisfactory.

Another ancillary Turbo problem was that of the oil pump required with the dry sump layout. This undergoes great strain, as we have heard elsewhere from Tony Rudd, and there were cases of tolerances at the joint faces going beyond acceptable limits, leading to a tightness in the bearing housing and uneven wear. Thus oil pressure should be checked carefully when the engine is hot. In general the Lotus 16-valve engine does use a lot of oil by modern standards and you should not be perturbed if consumption ranges between 300 and 500 miles per pint, maybe as low as 250 mpp in hard use, in either the Turbo or normal Esprit.

Overall

It has been a pleasure to write the story of such an interesting car. In an age of conformity the Esprit is a genuine character capable of giving any intelligent driver unmatched pleasure. It still has design faults—air conditioning is a must in the view of many Esprit connoisseurs—but through it all emerges the image of a true eighties sports car. Capable of giving tremendous cornering pleasure at 20 or 120 mph, and able to thread through

The Jenvey 2 litre Esprit at Brands Hatch in August 1979, where it qualified 12th fastest in a World Championship round of 32 qualifiers but failed to finish after another troubled outing. In 1982 British club racing the Esprit Turbo arrived and began a season long campaign in production sports car racing with considerable success

normal traffic with enormous safety margins and reassuring mpg figures. It is *not* a product manufactured merely to supply a computer-predicted market, but a clear illustration of a young and competitive company getting to grips with today's realities of pleasurable motoring. The fibreglass body and innumerable detail ingenuities, like using the robust internal roll-over hoop as a mounting point for strong door locks, are signatures of genius, just as surely as the Giugiaro imprint on every Esprit.

specifications

All figures are from Lotus, except where indicated, and should be read in conjunction with text, particularly those regarding performance and fuel economy.

Type: **Lotus Esprit Series 1**

Series production run: June 1976–May 1978

Total produced: 994

Body/chassis: GRP Lotus injection moulded body with style and cockpit by Giugiaro over steel backbone chassis with tubular frame engine bay construction. Integral rollover hoop, marine ply bulkhead and aluminium safety beams in doors. Majority of S1 production used self-colour body process.

Layout: Two door, two seat, mid-mounted engine, North–South with clutch and gearbox inline.

Engine: Lotus Type 907. Inline 4 cylinder with 45° cylinder block slant. Aluminium die-cast construction of 16-valve, DOHC, cylinder head and block. Wet sump lubrication, five main bearings. Twin Dell'Orto DHLA45E double choke carburettors, compression ratio 9.5:1. Bore × stroke, 95.2 mm × 62.9 mm for 1973 cc. Maximum power, 160 bhp at 6200 rpm. Peak torque, 140 lb ft. at 4900 rpm.

Electrical systems: Champion N7Y plugs; SU electrical fuel pump; sealed beam Lucas 75/60 watt quadruple 5 in. headlamps; negative earth Lucas 18ACR45 ampere alternator with 12v/50 ampere-hour battery. Lamps raised by single electric motor and transfer shaft.

Transmission: Citroën SM transaxle assembly with Lotus split bellhousing. Hydraulic operation of $8\frac{1}{2}$ in. diameter single plate clutch. Five speed all synchromesh gearbox with Citroën gears to Lotus ratio requirements (mph per 1000 rpm in brackets): First, 2.92:1 (5.69 mph); Second, 1.94:1 (8.56 mph); Third, 1.32:1 (12.58 mph); Fourth, 0.97:1 (17.15 mph); Fifth, 0.76:1 (21.85 mph). Final drive, 4.35:1. Maximum speed in gears (at 7300 rpm): First, 41.5 mph; Second, 62.5 mph; Third, 91.8 mph; Fourth, 125.2 mph; Fifth, 138 at 6300 rpm.

Suspension: Front, Opel Ascona-based unequal length pressed steel wishbones and inclined Armstrong shock absorber with Lotus coil spring, plus anti-roll bar. Camber $0-\frac{1}{2}°$; alignment, 3–5 mm toe in. Rear, Lotus fabricated with diagonal trailing arm and transverse single lower link. Fixed length driveshafts, inclined Armstrong damper/Lotus coil spring unit. Camber: $0-\frac{1}{2}°$; alignment, 8–10 mm toe in.

Steering: Rack and pinion, 3.1 turns lock to lock. Large diameter two-spoke steering wheel with Lotus imprinted in spokes. Castor, $3°-3\frac{1}{2}°$; kingpin, $9°$.

Wheels and tyres: Wolferace four bolt, chrome finish aluminium. Tyres, likely to be Dunlop SP Supersport. Front 6J × 14 in. diameter with 195/60*HR14. Rear, 7J × 14 in. with 205/70HR14. Pressures, 18 lb front; 28 lb rear.

Brakes: Dual circuit, servo-assisted, all disc (rear inboard) with system split front and rear. Front, 9.7 in. diameter. Rear, 10.6 in.

Dimensions: Length, 165 in.; wheelbase, 96 in.; height, 43.75 in.; width, 73.25 in.; front and rear tracks, 59.5 in.; ground clearance 5.5 in.; boot capacity 7 cu ft.; fuel tank capacity (two separate tanks, total), 15 Imperial gallons; weight (kerb): 1980 lb.

Initial price: £5844.13.

Claimed Performance

Speed (mph)	Seconds		
0–30	2.4	0–80	12.0
0–40	3.3	0–90	16.1
0–50	4.9	0–100	20.7
0–60	6.8	0–$\frac{1}{4}$ mile	15.0
0–70	9.1	Mpg (overall touring): 28	
		Max speed: 138	

*Lotus literature said 70 per cent aspect ratio but later production and demonstrators had 205/60 per cent low profile tyres fitted front and 205/70 per cent on the rear only.

Type: **Lotus Esprit Series 2**

Series production run: June 1978–January 1980

Total produced: 980

Body/chassis: As Series 1 except for: blade front spoiler replaced with wrap-around spoiler feeding larger radiator. Matt black paint highlights spoiler, sills, rear valance with double coachline from nose to tail. Series 2 decalling by fuel fillers and Rover 3500 ridged tail lights replace original inset units. Prominent collector ducts behind rear side windows.

Interior: revised instrument binnacle with black face/white numerals by Smiths and slide switches replace former black plastic rocker action. Seats 2 in. wider and redesigned engine cover incorporate Britool kit in hinged inspection lid.

Layout: As Series 1

Engine: As Series 1 but with air feed direct to carburettors and around engine bay. Power and torque figures officially the same although adoption of E-camshaft helps mid-range power curve during production run. Revised exhaust system.

Electrical systems: As Series 1 except: Motorola 55 ampere alternator; 9 fuses instead of 4; dual motors to raise quadruple Lucas H4 Halogen headlights; Stritone horns; digital clock; fibre optic illumination for switchgear functions.

124

Transmission: As Series 1

Suspension: As Series 1

Wheels and tyres: Italian Speedline four bolt, four spoke. Tyres, as later S1 (spare 185/70HR13). Wheel dimensions, 7JK × 14 in. front and 7½JK × 14 in. rear.

Steering: As Series 1

Dimensions: As Series 1 except for: Rear track, 60 in. instead of 59.5 in. and ground clearance 6 in. instead of 5.5 in.; weight up to 2248 lb.

Initial price: £11,124.37

Claimed Performance

Speed (mph)	Seconds
0–30	2.4
0–40	3.5
0–50	5.2
0–60	6.8
0–70	9.2
0–80	11.7
0–90	15.1
0–100	19.4

Standing ¼ mile: 15 seconds

Fuel consumption: Urban, 18.6 mpg; at constant 56 mph, 37.7 mpg; at a constant 75 mph, 31.3 mpg.

Gear speeds (at 7000 rpm): First, 40 mph; Second, 60 mph; Third, 88 mph; Fourth, 120 mph; Fifth, 138 mph at 6300 rpm.

Type: **Lotus Essex Commemorative Esprit Turbo and Turbo Esprit**

Series production run: June 1980–

Total produced: 173 (as at December 1981)

Body/chassis: Separately painted Lotus GRP, injection moulded. As for Series 2 except: new front and rear spoiler sections, new lower sills incorporating NACA ducts and air management system to engine bay and rear; new top lip above rear screen, rear slats. New tailgate with external boot lock. New chassis with box front section widened to take replacement Lotus front suspension. Full width radiator of increased capacity and oil cooler. New space frame for engine and transmission with four point mounting and increased torsional stiffness. Galvanised chassis with five year warranty and new rear suspension pick-up points.

Layout: As Series 1 but with single AiResearch T3 turbocharger aft of mid-mounted engine.

Engine: Lotus Type 910. Inline 4 cylinders, enlarged on 907 base, retaining alloy construction (but with dry sump lubrication), DOHC and 16-valve layout. Modifications include increased water cooling capacity, 7.5:1 cr and twin Dell'Orto 40DHLA double choke carburettors pressurised by Garrett AiResearch T3 turbocharger; maximum boost 8 psi. Bore × stroke, 95.2 mm × 76.2 mm for 2172 cc. Maximum power, 210 bhp at 6000 rpm. Peak torque, 200 lb ft. at 4000 rpm. Main bearing panel, camshafts, valves (including

125

Sodium filled exhausts), valve springs, pistons, water pump unique to Turbo amongst other detail items.

Electrical systems: Lucas 4PF fuel pump set to provide 4.5 psi excess over boost pressure at carburettor inlet with fuel return line to enlarged fuel tanks. Alternator, 70 ampere; 12 v 44 Ah battery; 8 fuses and quadruple 5.75 in. diameter Halogen lamps of 55/60 W rating. NGK BP6RES spark plugs.

Transmission: As Series 1 but with 9.5 in. diameter clutch plate and plunging constant velocity jointed driveshafts. Larger wheels and tyres allow 22.7 mph per 1000 rpm in fifth.

Suspension: Front, adapted from the Elite Eclat with Lotus fabricated upper wishbones, single lower link, anti-roll bar and coil spring/Armstrong shock absorber units. Track increased by one inch. Rear, as S1 and S2 except for upper lateral link to take over driveshaft top link duties. New aluminium hub carriers and 0.7 in. track increase.

Steering: As S1 and S2 except for 13.75 in. diameter steering wheel.

Wheels and tyres: Early cars on Compomotive 3-piece, current specification BBS Mahle light alloy, 7 in. × 15 in. front and 8 in. × 15 in. rear. Tyres, only Goodyear NCT with 195/60VR15 front and 235/60VR15 rear and 185/70 spare. Recommended pressures, 21 psi front and 25 psi rear.

Brakes: Servo-assisted with S2 later series 10.8 in. solid rear discs (still inboard) and bigger 10.5 in. solid front discs. Front and rear system split, as before.

Dimensions: Wheelbase as before (96 in.) and length (106 in.) but height 44 in.; width 73 in.; front track 60.5 in. and rear track 61.2 in. Ground clearance 5 in. Total fuel tank capacity 19 gallons. Weight (mid-laden), 2690 lb.

Initial price: £20,950

Claimed Performance (*Autocar* figures in brackets)

Speed (mph)	Seconds
0–30	2.05 (2.3)
0–40	2.85 (3.2)
0–50	4.20 (4.7)
0–60	5.55 (6.1)
0–70	7.35 (8.3)
0–80	9.25 (10.3)
0–90	11.85 (13.0)
0–100	14.65 (17.0)

Standing ¼ mile: 14.4 seconds at 98 mph (14.6s at 94 mph)

Fuel consumption: Urban, 19.7 mpg; at a constant 56 mph, 38.7 mpg; at a constant 75 mph, 33.3 mpg. *Autocar*/ECE lab figures in equivalent tests were: 15.7; 28.4 and 24.1 mpg.

Maximum speeds in gears (at 7300 rpm): First, 41.2 mph; Second, 62 mph; Third, 91.1 mph; Fourth, 123.5 mph; Fifth, 152 mph at 6700 rpm approx. *Autocar* **gear speeds** (at 7000 rpm): First, 39 mph; Second, 62 mph; Third, 91 mph; Fourth, 125 mph; Fifth, 149 mph at 6600 rpm.

Type: **Lotus Esprit Series 2.2**

Series production run: February 1980–March 1981

Total produced: 46

Body/chassis: As Series 2, but with galvanised chassis (S2) and Series 2.2 decalling on front and by fuel fillers.

Layout: As for Series 1 and 2

Engine: Type 912, enlarged from previous 2-litre with longer crankshaft stroke and strengthened bottom end. Main features as previously, but 9.4:1 compression. Bore × stroke, 95.25 mm × 76.20 mm for a capacity of 2172 cc. Peak power, 160 bhp at 6500 rpm. Maximum torque, 160 lb ft. at 5000 rpm.

Electrical system: Electronic ignition, some with 70 ampere alternator, otherwise as the S2.

Transmission: As Series 2 except: uprated clutch; flexible flywheel and performance claimed on 4:1 final drive (all other Esprits, 4.375:1).

Suspension, steering, wheels, tyres: As Series 2

Brakes: As later Series 2 with 9.7 in. diameter front discs and 10.8 in. rear.

Dimensions: As Series 2

Claimed performance: Contained in Series 2.2 Chapter 6, except for gear speeds. First, 40 mph; Second, 60 mph; Third, 88 mph; Fourth, 120 mph; Fifth, 138 mph.

Type: **Lotus Esprit Series 3**

Series production run: April 1981–

Total produced: 185 (to December 1981)

Body/chassis: GRP Lotus injection moulded body over Turbo type chassis and suspension. S3 differs from S2.2 visually in that previous matt black areas (front spoiler, sills etc) are painted in body colour with wrap round bumpers (carrying LOTUS motif embossed in rear bumper) and thin black coachline. Decalling to rear of back wheels and on bonnet identified S3, plus new air scoop/extractors behind rear windows and standard fitment of external locking filler caps. Revised cockpit trim and soundproofing.

Layout: As Series 1, 2, and S2.2

Engine: As S2.2 except for: one piece lid engine access; revised silencing for induction system; flexible joints for exhaust and revised air management system including part-reliance on convection principles to keep air moving when vehicle stationary.

Electrical systems: Motorola 70 ampere alternator standard; eight fuses; breakerless electronic ignition; quad halogen headlamps, as Turbo. Spark plugs protected by clip-in lightweight suppressor shield.

Transmission: As for Turbo but with two wheel and tyre choices to change gearing. On standard equipment Speedline mph per 1000 rpm figure is as for Series 2. On popular BBS Mahle/Goodyear option, gearing as for Turbo.

Suspension: As for Turbo, but lower poundage coil springs.

Steering: As for Turbo, including 13.75 in. diameter steering wheel saving one inch over previous non-Turbo models. Lotus figures for steering and suspension set up: Castor, 3°; Kingpin, 9.5°; Ratio: 15.4:1 in conjunction with front and rear suspension set at −0.5°. Camber ±15′: Lotus build-in 20 per cent anti-squat at the rear but no anti-dive characteristic.

Brakes: As for Turbo with 10.5 in. diameter solid disc fronts and 10.8 in. solid disc rear. Front–rear split of dual circuit maintained with vacuum servo-assistance.

Wheels and tyres: Standard Speedline four spoke as for S2.2 with 7 in. front and 7½ in. rear and 14 in. diameter. Optional BBS Mahle 15 in. diameter with 7 in. front width and 8 in. rear. Standard tyres as per S2.2 (205/60VR14 front and 205/70VR14 rear) but exclusively Goodyear NCT. Optional NCTs for 15 in. diameter option: 195/60VR15 and 235/60VR15. Get-you-home spare, 175/70SR14 limited to 60 mph. Pressures for standard 205s, 20 psi (F) and 27 psi (R). For optional 15 in. NCTs, 21 psi (F) and 25 psi (R).

Dimensions: As for previous non-Turbo Esprits but with track dimensions as for Turbo with optional BBS Mahle wheels. Weight, approximately 2400 lb.
Initial price: £13,461.23.

Claimed performance (secondary figures, courtesy *Autocar*, London)

Speed (mph)	Seconds (Lotus)	Seconds (*Autocar*)
0–30	2.4	2.3
0–40	3.5	3.5
0–50	5.0	5.0
0–60	6.7	6.7
0–70	8.9	9.6
0–80	11.3	12.4
0–90	14.8	16.1
0–100	19.2	20.9
¼ mile	—	15.5 at 88 mph

Gear speeds	Mph (Lotus)	Mph (*Autocar*)
First	40	41 at 7000 rpm
Second	60	62 at 7000 rpm
Third	88	91 at 7000 rpm
Fourth	120	124 at 7000 rpm
Fifth	138	135 at 5950 rpm

* *Autocar* test vehicle OPW 666W on optional 15 in. diameter wheels.

Fifth gear performance

Speed (mph)	Seconds (Lotus)	Seconds (*Autocar*)
30–50	13.0	10.4
50–70	8.4	9.9
70–90	8.3	11.2
80–100	8.6	12.9

Fuel consumption (*Autocar* S2 versus S3 comparison)

Constant speed (mph)	Series 2	Series 3
30	29.8	35.8
50	33.2	30.6
70	28.2	24.6
100	21.2	19.3

*Note, overall Lotus claims were justified for fuel saving of bigger engine as *Autocar* got 21.7 mpg, over 10 per cent better than they managed in S2.

Esprit production

Supplied by Lotus Cars on January 15, 1982 and superseding earlier figures.

S1	994	June 76–May 78
S2	980	June 78–Jan 80
S2.2	46	Feb 80–Mar 81
S3	185	Apr 81–To Date (Dec 81)
Turbo	173	June 80–To Date (Dec 81)
Total	2378	June 1976–Dec 1981

Percentage split Home/Export: 50/50

Esprit changes 1976–1982: A factory list

Spoiler: S1 lip spoiler
S2/2.2/3 full width wrap around section. S2/2.2 Black Hammerite.
S3 body colour

Bumpers: S1/2 ABS moulded. S3 GFRP wrap around with LOTUS logo moulded into rear
. . . same bumpers as Turbo.

Air Scoops: behind side windows: S1 none. S2/2.2 inlet only. S3 inlet and air extraction from trailing face. All versions matt black. S3 body colour.

Side Sills: S1/2 same shape: S1 in body colour S2/2.2 in black Hammerite. S3 new shape with lip on bottom edge—painted body colour to match nose spoiler.

Silencer cover panel: S1 'solid' in body colour. S2/2.2/3 incorporate moulded air slats— body colour.

Door Mirrors: Fixed pod on S1. Electric remote with chrome stem initial S2. Late S2 and JPS Commemorative and S3 same remote but with fixed stem all matt black.

Rear Lights: S1 Recessed lenses from Fiat X1/9.
S2/2.2/3 proud fitting Rover type with black bezel surrounds. Number plate housing on S1 recessed—S2/2.2/3 proud fit with black bezel.

Road Wheels: S1 Wolfrace polished alloy. S2/2.2/3 Speedline silver paint only. S3 option of BBS only with Turbo tyre sizes.

Engine Bay: S1 Engine cover one piece moulding. Late S1 had oil/water hinged access hatch.
S2 Engine cover redesigned with tool kit compartment on top, access hatch at rear of cover. Engine cover was finished in Hammerite and part trimmed with carpet.
S2 Engine cover also incorporated air trunking; from LH external air intake to carbs—hot air from engine bay thermal extraction via air trunking from right hand wall of engine cover to RH external 'ear'. US models had electric motor fan boost for extraction.
S3. Engine bay now 'walled' with full width removable lid. S3 'ears' used for inlet to carbs *and* exhausting of engine bay heat.

Battery Location: S1 Below rearmost side window.
S2 Recessed into floor of boot (bottom right)
S3/Turbo rear corner—RH—behind wheelarch

Brakes: S1 through to 2.2   F 9.8 in. R 10.8 in.
S3/Turbo   F 10.5 in. R 10.8 in.

Clutch: S1 through to 2.2   8.5 in.
S3/Turbo   9.5 in.

Headlamp Lift: S1 launched with single motor lift. Changed during production (with service mod. available for earlier version) to twin motor. System used through S2/2.2/3 and Turbo. Reason for changes to twin motors: Long tie bar between left and right lamp pods allowed too much flexing and subsequent fluttering of lights on rough terrain also single motor struggled to retract lamps over 120 mph.

Chassis: S1/2/2.2 remained same in the metal. Only significant change being introduction of galvanised hot dip treatment on S2.2
Completely new Turbo chassis and suspension adopted for S3.

Gear Change: S1/2/2.2 remained unchanged with 3 sections in linkage along left hand side of engine.
S3 (Turbo) 2 sections in linkage along right hand side of engine—more positive feeling.

Radiator: S1 aluminium core to copper with 1×10 in. fan then 2×10 in. S2 changed to Elite type radiator with 2×11 in. fans.

Interior Heater: S1 improved during production carried over to S2. Early S2 saw our own designed unit in production—still current on S3.
Air conditioning option during S2—through to current.

Exhaust Systems: Intermediate silencer and flanged joints instead of slide joints introduced S2.
Late S2 and current 3 ball jointed down pipes (Stainless steel).
S3 flexible downpipes with ball joints and flexible section before silencer.

Interior: S1 Tartan plaid, green and red. Veglia instruments—green faces. Large ashtray on centre tunnel. Window lift switches on top of centre tunnel either side of choke lever.
S2 instruments changed to Smiths—black faces/white digits. Switchgear changed to fibre optic back lit paddle type. Window lift switches moved down into gear level tray area. Small ashtrays (2) flush fitted on door sills.
S2 seats modified with lowered hip-point and reshaped foam foundations.
S3 as Turbo.
S2 header rail above windscreen changed to include digital clock.

Acknowledgements

My debt to the senior staff of Lotus Cars is quite simply that such an honest account of the glamorous Esprit's life would not have been possible without their co-operation. At this level Lotus are amongst the best in the world for a writer to work with, as the company's size leaves decision-making management still accessible to mortals below.

Primarily I must say a hearty 'thanks a lot' to Donovan 'Don Mac' McLauchlan. As the Lotus Public Relations one man band Don gets a fair bit of stick from a demanding management and a frustrated queue of journalists wanting to borrow the only demonstrator—which happens to be earning its keep elsewhere most of the time! Don always responded to phone calls and made it possible for me to gather some of the frank comments you will find within from Mike Kimberley, Tony Rudd, Colin Spooner and many others (including Colin Chapman on an earlier occasion) when they mostly needed to be packed and off to Japan the next day . . . literally. Over the years I have also listened with pleasure to Roger Putnam at Lotus and was glad to renew that association.

I must also express my gratitude to Ray Hutton, editor of *Autocar*, who generously let me use some of that magazine's data to bring me up to date.

In the sixties and early seventies I co-built a Lotus Seven S3 and the fibreglass S4. The enjoyment I had from those cars, and the road test Elans and Europas, lives on honourably in the Esprit. I admire both the company that created them and the product today, but I hope that has not prevented my writing a useful book for anyone—potential owner onwards—interested in this arresting blend of Italian style and British technology.

For the photographs I am indebted to Mirco Decet who not only shot many himself but who also assembled the rest of the collection. Other contributors were Bell and Colvill Ltd., East Horsley; Focalpoint, Norwich; Keith Hamshere; Don McLauchlan of Lotus Cars, Hethel; Rich McCormack of The Newport Press, Santa Ana; Steve Yarnell.

Index